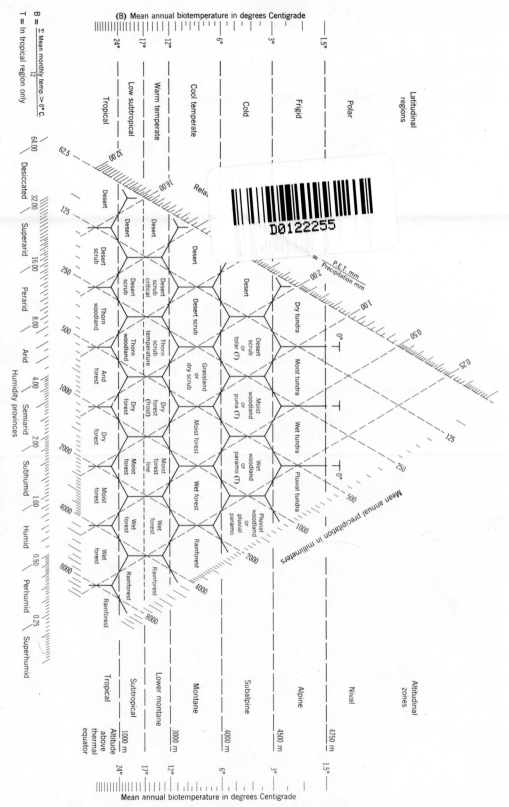

Figure 3.3. Holdridge system of classification of the world plant formations and life zones.[4]

WILDLIFE BIOLOGY

21-9-
3-4-5

WILDLIFE BIOLOGY

SECOND
EDITION

Raymond F. Dasmann

University of California, Santa Cruz

JOHN WILEY & SONS

NEW YORK   CHICHESTER   BRISBANE   TORONTO

Cover & Interior Design: Angie Lee
Cover Photo: Nelson Kniffen-Shostal Assoc.
Photo Research by Teri Leigh Stratford
Photo Editor, Stella Kupferberg

Library of Congress Cataloging in Publication Data:

Dasmann, Raymond Fredric, 1919–
  Wildlife biology

  Bibliography: p.
  Includes index.
  1. Animal ecology. 2. Wildlife management.
I. Title.

QH541.D36 1981   591.5   80-19006
ISBN 0-471-08042-X

Printed in the United States of America

10 9 8 7 6 5 4 3 2 1

PREFACE

For reasons more or less beyond my control, 16 years have passed since the first edition of *Wildlife Biology* was published. During that time, slowly but inevitably, certain portions of the book have become outdated. New findings have become available, research has gone on, management experience has accumulated. Meanwhile, I have worked in many parts of the world, frequently on problems related to wildlife, but often on broader environmental issues. It is inevitable, I suppose, that my perspective would change, and questions that seemed important to me when viewed from the safe interior of the United States seemed less important when seen from some other part of the world. I suspect also that this experience has made me somewhat less inclined to be dogmatic.

This second edition is different in many ways from the first. Some of the changes are obvious; I have dropped some sections and added others. Other changes may be less apparent unless one reads it carefully—some of my yes statements have been changed to no's or maybe's. A lot of old examples are there because I like them, but I've added the results of new studies. I have tried to keep this a short book, since too many books resemble in their various editions the evolution of dinosaurs. Small books are cheaper, and there is a better chance that somebody will read them from cover to cover, even at one sitting, which is best. That means, of course, that I have left things out that some teachers will believe to be more important than the things I have put in. I can't help that; there is no way to include everything. I have tried to keep this book nonmathematical and suited to beginning students or nonstudents. Partly this is because I like words better than symbols. I have been somewhat resistant to new terminology, except where it expresses an innovative idea that one cannot cover with old words, and I've also tried to avoid too much jargon.

This book is really part of my continuing effort to make the world a better place for wild animals and people. I have a great indebtedness to wildlife. Deer, and impala, coyotes, and kangaroos have helped pay for my education and have supported me most of my life. I owe them a lot.

Raymond F. Dasmann

CONTENTS

WILDLIFE BIOLOGY

1

WHAT GOOD ARE WILD ANIMALS?

Somewhere in times beyond memory the species that was to call itself human appeared on this planet, and, like all species, learned to distinguish its own kind from all other species on earth. When spoken language took an elaborate form, the first humans no doubt learned words to describe the world around them but I wonder if they had any word for wild since *all* the world was wild. Except in a few places, the world was to remain wild, and most people everywhere continued to live as one species among many—stronger and fiercer than some, weaker than others, but not presuming any dominance or control. But in those few places, ideas were to take root that would bring power to those who pursued them. A distinction was made between species for whose care humans were responsible and all others, between the tame and the wild.

In the *Oxford Universal Dictionary*, which the English attach some importance to, there is no word for wildlife. In *Webster's,* more commonly used in America, wildlife is defined as "living things that are neither human nor domesticated; esp: mammals, birds, and fishes hunted by man." In more recent years, in order to communicate with their relatives across the Atlantic, the English have started to use the word wildlife. However, in crossing the ocean, words seem to shed some of their meaning, and only the first part of *Webster's* definition made the journey. The result is that in England people have started to talk about plants or vegetation as wildlife, whereas in America, in the recent definitive book *Wildlife and America* (Brokaw, 1978), wildlife is stated to be only animals. In this book, the emphasis will be on birds and mammals, but with some attention to the other animals with backbones: fish, reptiles, and amphibians. In American usage, wildlife is sometimes viewed in the same sense as game, and excludes fish. Thus we have a Fish and Wildlife Service with the same functions on a federal level as a Fish and Game Department on the state level. But game does signify that the creatures involved are hunted for or fished for sport. These species will receive more emphasis in this book since they are the ones we seem to know the most about. There are many volumes about the group of species we call deer, but very few about the group that we call chipmunks, although ounce for ounce (or gram for gram) a chipmunk is just as important as a deer.

Since people started to dwell in towns and cities many of them have lost touch with—and some seem even to have forgotten—that there is something called wild nature beyond the city boundaries. Wildlife means little to them, and they find it difficult to understand those who think it important. So when a little fish is used as a reason to prevent the construction of a big dam or a salamander diverts the route of a freeway, these people think that insanity is spreading among their fellow humans and write bitter editorials or speak from the legislature floor. But city people are not the only ones who lack consideration for any creature not of direct economic concern. European conservation societies have tried for decades to get the Italian, French, and Belgian peasantry to stop netting song birds—but the people who are the culprits believe that creatures that clearly belong to nobody belong to anybody who wants to put them in the pot. Once eaten, they are an internal affair. The birds that migrate each year from Europe to Africa must run a gauntlet in the Mediterranean countries, where many a gun is turned against them, regardless of conservation laws and international treaties.

In the opening of his book *A Sand County Almanac,* Aldo Leopold, one of the founders of American wildlife management, states simply: "There are some who can live without wild things and some who cannot. These essays are the delights and dilemmas of one who cannot." More recently, as we learn more about the ecology of planet earth, we can question whether anyone can live without wild things. We have learned that all life on earth is one, that all living things are tied together in intricate networks of life and nonlife that we call ecosystems. Science is coming closer to the earlier visions of poets and mystics. We don't yet know enough about how humankind and natural systems are tied together, but we do realize that until we learn how things operate we had better save all the parts. Still, there are many people who do not know much about wildlife or ecology, and more who are willing to grant their importance, in a general sense, so long as it does not interfere with their own process of earning a living, or accumulating wealth, power, prestige or whatever they think is worth accumulating. And so it seems necessary to spell out some of the ways in which wildlife is important.

WILDLIFE VALUES

When a coyote, jackal, wolf, or hyena begins to howl around the flocks or herds of a pastoralist (call the individual a cowboy or sheepherder in America), the value of that particular kind of wildlife seems totally negative to the human involved. When a school of fish entangles itself in the nets spread out by a fishing boat, its value is all positive. When a hunter in the Canadian Rockies encounters his first bighorn ram, staring at him from a nearby rock, its value seems infinite. A mockingbird in the back garden, an eagle soaring, a giraffe moving across the plains, or a dolphin playing in the surf can have values to the observer that cannot fit anybody's economic yardstick.

Commercial Value

The commercial value of wildlife is best seen in the world's marine fisheries, yielding perhaps 70 million tons of food, a good percentage of the world's animal protein, and for many people the only animal protein they can hope to afford. Its cash value is in billions of dollars. It yields a way of life to those who fish and to those who process, prepare, transport, and sell fish and fish products. Yet it is a value provided entirely by wild stocks toward which humans retain a hunter-gatherer relationship, doing little or nothing to enhance the natural production. What is called marine fisheries management is not management in the usual sense; it is an attempt to control the amount of fish taken, and includes research to try to determine what is going on among the fish involved. Although there is talk about mariculture (the rearing and care of marine life), except for a few species in a few places, there is little of it being done.

Converting wildlife into money. Fish meal produced from the anchovies of the Humboldt Current, Paracas, Peru.

Other than fish, the commercial value of many forms of marine life has long been recognized: sea mammals, sea turtles, shellfish, and a whole range of other invertebrates all have had a cash value attached to them and have attracted those who pursue them for money. This has been fatal to some—the species have been exterminated—and threatening to many others. It has in turn provided a way of life for many who call themselves biologists, managers, conservationists, or other terms and who seek to preserve these wild species.

Freshwater fish and other aquatic life of the continents have a direct commercial value in many countries and provide large amounts of food for people. These species form the base for much of the aquaculture that is going on, which in some countries has become one of the most efficient ways of using land or water in terms of the quantity and value of the animal protein produced. However, such aquaculture depends on wild stocks—the species reared are not truly domesticated.

The commercial value of the wild animal life of dry land is

more easily overlooked. For the so-called "primitive" people of the world (meaning those who have not enlisted in the global economy), it is often their principal base of animal food. Even among the cash economies of the world, wild animal life makes a considerable contribution to the monetary value of wild foods consumed. Fur-bearing animals unwillingly support an entire industry—the fur trade—which in its turn has endangered the existence of many species, while increasing the quantity, but not the quality of life, of those reared on fur farms. Trade in live animals provides a means of support for many people who cater to people's desire to own strange or exotic pets, or who supply the demands of scientific or educational institutions. Some species have had such a high economic value placed on certain of their parts that their future has been threatened: the ivory of elephants, the horns of rhinoceros, the glands of musk deer, the antlers of deer—all command high prices in the market.

Some studies in Africa and elsewhere indicate that wild animal life can be more productive and economically profitable than domesticated animal life would be on the same ground. This is particularly true of the so-called marginal lands, those not well suited to farm or pasture. There is also evidence that many wild animal species could profitably be domesticated and would prove more useful than many domestic breeds in some environments (Dasmann, 1964).

But wildlife has its negative economic values that often become much too obvious to farmer or rancher. Elephants in African gardens, deer in the almond orchard, great flocks of starlings in the farmlands, or just a few wild predators in the pasturelands can cause serious economic losses. Balancing losses and gains, eliminating or controlling negative effects while enhancing positive values have become in some countries the task of wildlife agencies and are part of the work called wildlife management.

Game Value

In many countries and particularly in those inhabited by European peoples, wildlife has a higher economic value than what can be realized from the direct sale of its meat or hides. This is its worth as game, a recreational value to those who hunt or fish for

sport. In the United States, many millions of people hunt or fish
and spend billions of dollars in pursuit of their sport. Many busi-
nesses cater to their needs by producing firearms or fishing tackle,
camping equipment, recreational vehicles, or by providing accom-
modation or food and drink. In the wilder parts of the country, the
principal local industry is tourism, and a prime reason for tourists
to visit is the enjoyment of hunting or fishing. The demands of
these people for wildlife or fish is sufficient so that large blocks of
public land are reserved for their recreational use, and many private landowners have found it profitable to cater to their needs.
High-value farming lands have often been sold to provide space
for still higher-value hunting clubs. Sport hunters and fishers in
America have in general been conservation minded. Through their
purchase of licenses and payment of other fees they have provided
the principal support for state wildlife conservation agencies. In
their organized associations they have been active both politically
and directly in wildlife conservation, and have shown willingness
to give up hunting entirely when a species becomes endangered, or
they believe it might be. Nevertheless, by the nature of their sport,
hunters in particular generate opposition from a growing number
of people who dislike the killing of any wild animal except in case
of direct human need. These people in turn incur the dislike of the
sportsmen, and adjudicating the clash between the two provides
an interesting challenge for those charged with public responsibility for wildlife management.

Aesthetic Values

If wildlife had no other value and were an economic detriment, it would still be worth preserving, for many people, for its
sheer beauty and appeal to the human spirit. People with city
gardens often put out great effort to attract birds, just so they can
watch and hear them. Ornithological societies, or just plain bird
watchers, have become a numerous breed in many countries and
are a major force for wildlife conservation. People go to national
parks to watch or photograph animals in the wild and thus provide income for all those who cater to their needs. In many developing countries with limited economical potential but large areas
of wild land, the world tourist trade can be a principal source of
foreign exchange, and much of this is attracted by wildlife—

whether it is the marine life of a coral reef or the herds of game on the African plains. Money brought into an economy by people who come to see wild creatures goes into segments of the economy that seem to have no direct relation to wildlife.

In the United States the value of wild animals as game has often been measured economically and is impressively high. Worldwide it is the aesthetic value of wild places and animal life that becomes more important and provides an economic justification for marine reserves, national parks, and wildlife refuges.

Ethical Values

To some the main reason for protecting nature is that we have an obligation to do so; we have no right to destroy wild species. In the earlier religions of humankind, many of which still continue, a reverence and respect for wild animals was common. Coyote might be an animal yapping in the hills, but Coyote was also a spirit one would do well not to offend if one happened to be a California Indian. In many cultures dependent on hunting, the hunter was careful to show the proper veneration for the spirit of the animal being hunted—to ignore it was to invite catastrophe. In the more recent world religions, many followers of Buddhism and Hinduism believe it wrong to take the life of an animal. In the Judaeo-Christian tradition, a tendency to see humanity as separate from nature has been common, but even Christianity had Saint Francis of Assisi who lived with and spoke to wild animals, or more recently Albert Schweitzer, who practiced and taught a "reverence for life."

· On the more scientific side, the ethical importance of wildlife has been stressed by Aldo Leopold, who pointed out that a "land ethic" does not prevent the alteration, management, or use of plants and animals, but "it does affirm their right to continued existence." A "land ethic" changes a person from a conqueror of the natural community to a "plain member and citizen of it." "It implies respect for his fellow-members and also respect for the community as such" (Leopold, 1949).

Scientific Values

The pursuit of science has led people to a knowledge and understanding of many of the earth's species and the ways in which they are related in an evolutionary sense, as well as how they interact to keep the planet habitable. A pursuit of knowledge, for its own sake, has its many spin-offs that are of direct value to humans. Sea urchins have helped develop an understanding of human embryology; a desert toad has helped in the early determination of pregnancy; rhesus monkeys have contributed toward an understanding of human blood groups, the antlers of deer have provided a means for measuring the degree of radioactive contamination of natural environments; studies of animal behavior have revealed new insights into the knots and ravels encountered by psychiatrists in their studies of the human mind. A chimpanzee learns to communicate by sign language, and a Japanese macaque somehow spreads the knowledge of how to wash sweet potatoes and we begin to have a new understanding of communication. Dolphins and whales talk away in their own language and we begin to wonder what they know that we do not. We do not know when some obscure wild animal will soar into prominence supplying some needed clue to human health and survival. Perhaps it may turn out as the California Indians once believed—that dolphins patrol the boundaries of the known world and keep it safe for humans.

Ecological Values

There are some who believe that ecology came into being in the 1960s and reached prominence with the first Earth Day celebration in 1970. The truth is rather different. Ecological knowledge provided a basis for the behavior of virtually all hunter-gatherers, most agriculturalists and pastoralists, and, until the rise of city civilization, most people on earth. It was not formalized, and not called ecology; it was simply an understanding of the way things work. Scientific ecology has been around for some centuries. Alexander von Humboldt made important contributions to this science in the days of Napoleon. Charles Darwin was a keen ecological observer. In the 1860s, Haeckel coined the word "oecology" for what was a recognized way of looking at things. In the United States, some of the early scientific ecologists influenced forest and land management and range management at the beginnings of the 20th century. Some of their errors are still perpetuated, along with the truths that they discovered. Nevertheless, ecology, as a way of looking at whole systems and examining the ways in which they operate is a relatively new arrival on the scientific scene. Its integrative approach, based on putting things together, differs from the "single vision" that has characterized much of science and depends on taking things apart and seeing how each part works. In the study of wildlife, the "reductionist" approach much of biology in the past exemplified has proved useful. By studying single species we learned a great deal about those species. But, when we began to manage those species, we learned that predictions based on their population behavior in isolation from other species, or in the presence of those few that we considered important enough, often proved wrong. We thought we could harvest a species at some "maximum sustainable yield" and get by with it. Whales were to teach us that we were wrong (May, *et al.,* 1979). Now, in the 1980s, human beings are attempting to learn the old rules, in a conscious way, that were used, almost unconsciously, to enable people to survive on this planet. Wildlife, so long studied, so little understood, is helping us to learn. Gary Snyder (1977) recognized this in his book *The Old Ways:*

> *The Cahuila Indians who lived in the Palm Springs desert and the mountains above gathered plants from valley floor to mountain peak with precise knowledge. They said not everybody will do it, but almost anybody can, if he pays enough attention and is patient, hear a little voice from plants. The Papago of southern Arizona said that a man who was humble and brave and persistent, would some night hear a song in his dream, brought by birds that fly in from the Gulf of California, or a hawk, a cloud, the wind, or the red rain spider; and that song would be his—would add to his knowledge and power.*

Those who would manage wildlife today must be "humble and brave and persistent" since we who have so much learning still know little, and it may well be that wild animals exist to give us the knowledge and the power to continue to live in harmony with our planet.

WILDLIFE AS A NATURAL RESOURCE

When I first started to write and be published on the subject of conservation twenty years ago, the world seemed a much simpler place. In those days all of us seemed to agree on various definitions that have since been revealed as less than adequate. Thus, natural resources were things provided by nature that were useful to humans, and we could neatly subdivide them into renewable and nonrenewable, essentially drawing the line between the living and nonliving—or between those that were constantly restored or provided by ongoing natural processes and those that were not. This same line of thinking led people to describe other people as "our most important natural resource." And then finally some philosopher or poet said, "Hey, let us not confuse people with things," and somebody else said, "let's not confuse our fellow beings, the wild animals, with things," and others extended this to plants, and somebody else said rocks are important too. What they were objecting to was the language and way of thinking of the economists, who like to reduce phenomena to measurable units so that we can begin to see their relative place in human economy. This has been a useful approach, but it may have been pushed too far.

Nevertheless, if we are dealing with people today who regard coal as a natural resource (which it is), then we must also point out that wildlife is a natural resource, by the same definition. It is valuable and useful to humanity, and its economic value, in part at least, can be measured. It is useful also to remember that wildlife is a *renewable* resource; with proper care and management—or if left strictly alone—it will reproduce itself. As long as the planet remains not too different from what it is today, we can continue to hunt and fish and still have animals to hunt or fish. But if we continue to use petroleum or coal, which are only very slowly renewable under conditions that now exist on our planet, that coal and petroleum will be gone—they are *nonrenewable* resources. But the boundaries between the two categories are not fixed and definite. All renewable resources depend on a continued flow of the nonliving (some would say nonrenewable) resources of the planet that circulate through ecosystems and sustain life. If the flow is interrupted, if those nonliving materials cease to be available—the nitrogen, the phosphorus, the aluminum, the iron, the water, and so on—then life is no longer renewable.

It was not more than a century ago that people believed all wild animals were destined inevitably to disappear under the advance of human populations and civilization. Conservation was seen as an effort to postpone the inevitable. It was a useful concept for people to recognize that humankind need not advance its own well-being at the expense of the natural world, that it was possible to cut wood and not destroy forests, to eat wild animals and not destroy wildlife, that a balance between human demands and the capacity of the wild world to produce could be reached. But that understanding has been slow in coming, and over much of the world it has not been reached at all. People are "mining" living communities as though they were inert substances of limited supply, on the principle that the first gets the most and the devil take the hindmost. The idea that they could be there for everybody forever and still supply our reasonable needs today has not reached the minds of those who permit their exploitation. And so we have reached a crisis of "natural resources," which is in fact a crisis of the *biosphere,* that layer of living and nonliving interacting components on the earth, of which we are all a part, and on which we all depend.

THE STATUS OF WILDLIFE CONSERVATION

When the first edition of this book appeared in 1964 I had the temerity to present a neat table summarizing the status of wildlife conservation around the world. I again present this table, not just for its historical interest, but as a point of reference. In one sense, much that is in it is still true. But other things have happened, and they are of frightening consequence, not really predictable at that time. When the first edition came out I was about to launch myself in a career concerned with international conservation. I have since seen many distant places and different kinds of country. I wish that what I had to report was encouraging.

To review Table 1.1, the first area of correction is *China,* where an interest in wild nature has persisted throughout all of the changes and turmoil. It is not just the giant panda that has been saved, but many wild ecosystems and natural communities. *South-eastern Asia* has grown worse, and the future seems even more bleak. *Africa* is in some ways much better. The enlightened attitudes called for have been realized in many governments, and Kenya, Tanzania, Zambia, and Mozambique, to name a few, have

Table 1.1   Status of Wildlife Conservation

Region	Status of Wildlife
Europe	*Satisfactory.* Great changes from prehistoric times, during which natural vegetation largely disappeared and most wildlife vanished. Remaining natural areas and wild animals are, in general, well cared for. Mediterranean region is exception; population pressure and poverty prevent effective restoration.
Soviet Union	*Satisfactory.* Serious efforts at conservation and restoration appear likely to repair past damage.
China	*Unsatisfactory.* Government attitude has been unfavorable. Severe past damage and extreme present population pressure.
Mediterranean Asia and Africa	*Unsatisfactory.* Extreme past damage. Little effective conservation today.
North America	*Generally satisfactory.* Wildlife changed and reduced during period of settlement. Wildlife conservation now effective, but threatened by rapid population growth.
Southeastern Asia	*Generally unsatisfactory.* Rapid population growth and governmental indifference is causing land deterioration and disappearance of natural vegetation. Many species near extinction.
Africa	*Unsatisfactory.* Efforts of colonial administrations at protection halted drastic changes of earlier

Table 1.1 (continued)

Region	Status of Wildlife
	times in some areas. At present all resources threatened by political turmoil and unbridled population growth. Future depends on adoption of enlightened attitudes by governments.
South America	• *Generally unsatisfactory.* Rapid population growth threatens future of large areas which previously were little affected.
Australia and New Zealand	*Satisfactory.* Period of unchecked exploitation and destruction of natural communities and animal life now seems halted. Enlightened conservation policies, confused somewhat in New Zealand by issue of exotic animals and their future.
Oceanic islands	› *Unsatisfactory.* Widespread destruction of natural areas and native wildlife.

done remarkably well at protecting wild areas and wild species. All are now caught in a population and economic crunch that does not bode well for the future. *South America* and Latin America generally have grown worse, but there are bright spots in Costa Rica and Peru, and their example may spread. *Oceanic islands,* in the Pacific (although not noticeably elsewhere) have taken a definite turn for the better; with some help from richer countries they may succeed in saving their natural heritage.

But overriding all these comments are certain global trends of serious consequence:

The destruction of the tropical rain forest and tropical humid forests in general, in which most species of land animals now live. This is a worldwide threat that could seriously endanger as much as one-quarter of all land species, if not all life on earth.

Aerial dusting of pesticides, California. The release of toxic chemicals into the environment represents a growing threat to wild animal life.

The growing spread of deserts into the drier lands of the world, and into regions that were not so dry.   This is bringing the elimination of a broad category of animal and plant species and is of the most serious consequence for human survival.

The widespread use of chemical substances for the control of animals and plants considered to be "pests," and the accidental or deliberate release of numerous other chemical substances, organic and inorganic, radioactive and otherwise, into the biosphere.   It is virtually impossible to keep up with the toxic substances, or potential toxins, now being released into the environment; it is even more difficult to measure their damage. These substances may have global effects—including destruction of the ozone screen of the atmosphere that now protects us from severe ultraviolet radiation, and climatic changes that can only be unfavorable to most existing forms of life—as well as more direct effects on the immediate survival of a wide range of species. We do not know what the effects will be. Perhaps if the process continues we will discover too late to do anything about it.

One who is concerned with wildlife biology and management is now involved with a process that includes much of human activity as well as the "natural" behavior of wild populations. There once was a time when those who were "fed up" with their fellow humans and their activities could go out and study wild animals, or thought that they could. In reality this was an illusion and they inevitably were caught up in human affairs. Now it is inescapable that they must get totally involved in the political, social, and economic life of their fellow humans.

2

THE TEN-THOUSAND
YEAR WAR

The story of the human species is still being worked on, pushed
back farther into time with the discovery of new branches of our
family tree. We may not learn the complete picture, but we know
that people have been around through some major changes on
earth and that some of the greatest changes have involved wild
animal populations. In North America some of the earliest human
remains are associated with the bones of an extinct Pleistocene
fauna: mammoths, mastodons, ground sloths, giant bears and
wolves, bigger condors, wild horses, and camels. Vegetation was
different and changed back and forth—from desert to savanna
and back to desert in the American southwest, for example. Ice
sheets were to move down from Canada into the northern United
States, and then retreat and come forward again. Hunting cultures
developed and people invented more effective weapons, but these
cultures were to disappear along with the larger mammals. To
what extent people were responsible for exterminating the Ice Age
fauna is not known, but it now seems unlikely that they had an
important role. However, when people moved into new areas of
North America, they were likely to have had disruptive effects on

the species already there. New species must adjust and adapt to new environments; in the process they can create considerable disturbance. We have seen such effects in recent times with animal species brought into North America—the English sparrow and starling have taken a long time to settle in, and there was a belief that they would displace and cause the extinction of many native birds. We have seen the effects also of the movement of the European culture into North America, although whether it has "settled in" remains in question.

At the time of European settlement, North America was inhabited by people who were basically hunter-gatherers, although in the east and southwest subsistence agriculture was also important and farther south in Mexico agriculture provided the principal support for the population. The hunter-gatherers appeared to have worked out a benign relationship with the animals and plants on which they depended for food—a relationship particularly obvious in California, a region that supported the highest human population density north of Mexico. The abundance of wildlife in Indian times has been commented on by many, but Margolin's (1978) summary is worth repeating:

> The early explorers and adventurers, no matter how well-travelled in other parts of the globe, were invariably struck by the plentiful animal life here. "There is not any country in the world which more abounds in fish and game of every description," noted the French sea captain, la Perouse. Flocks of geese, ducks, and seabirds were so enormous that when alarmed by a rifle shot they were said to rise "in a dense cloud with a noise like that of a hurricane." Herds of elk—"monsters with tremendous horns," as one of the early missionaries described them—grazed the meadowlands in such numbers that they were often compared with great herds of cattle. Pronghorn antelopes, in herds of one or two hundred, or even more, dotted the grassy slopes.
>
> Packs of wolves hunted the elk, antelope, deer, rabbits, and other game. Bald eagles and giant condors glided through the air. Mountain lions, bobcats, and coyotes—now seen only rarely—were a common sight. And of course there was the grizzly bear.

Margolin also quotes from the journals of many early visitors to California concerning the tameness of wild animals. The relationship with people was not one of fear or avoidance, even though people hunted animals regularly. It was more reminiscent of the balance one sees in Africa between lions and their prey. Antelope seem to ignore the large predators except when these are actually hunting, and once the hunt is over, the scene settles down again to one of mutual acceptance.

In earlier works I have attempted to describe the differences between people who live in one place and are dependent on the local ecosystem for their support and those who do not. If one is totally dependent, or largely so, on the animals and plants of a particular area, one must learn to maintain some reasonable balance. A people who exterminate the animals on which they depend for food will themselves starve, and the same would apply to plant species. It follows that people who have lived for centuries or longer in the same place, without major sources of supply from the outside, must develop some working relationship with the species surrounding them. I have called these people *ecosystem people* because they occupy one, or a few, local ecosystems and are dependent on them. There may be some trade with other peoples, but this does not supply the means of subsistence. Such people return what they use, sooner or later, back to the soils and waters on which they depend. Human wastes, and, in time, human bodies are recycled, their chemicals given back to the land to be used again by other species. There is no subtraction from the natural wealth of the area, except by slow natural processes of erosion.

Such people still exist in many parts of the world today, but they are becoming less numerous as they are blotted out by the spread of the prevailing global economy. There is every reason to believe that the original Americans were basically ecosystem people. When the Plains Indians were first encountered by United States travellers some disruption had occurred. The horse, introduced by the Spanish at the time of Cortez, had spread northward with Spanish settlements and was adopted by the Indians who in time became skilled riders (Farb, 1968). A new relationship was being worked out among people, horses, and the vast herds of bison that occupied the plains, and older balances had been upset. Nevertheless, it was possible for their spokesmen to describe the situation as follows:

We did not think of the great open plains, the beautiful rolling hills, and winding streams with tangled growth as "wild." Only to the white man was nature a "wilderness" and only to him was the land "infested" with "wild" animals and "savage" people. To us it was tame. Earth was bountiful and we were surrounded with the blessings of the Great Mystery. Not until the hairy man from the east came and with brutal frenzy heaped injustices upon us and the families we loved was it "wild" for us. When the very animals of the forest began fleeing from his approach, then it was that for us the "Wild West" began. (Chief Luther Standing Bear, Oglala Sioux, McLuhan, 1972)

I have described the "hairy man from the east" as belonging to a different basic cultural tradition. Not an ecosystem person, although he was descended from them before they in turn were disrupted by the spread of Roman civilization, but a member of what I have called *biosphere people.* Biosphere people are not dependent on the resources of one ecosystem, or a few local ecosystems. Through organized colonialism and trade they can draw on the resources of many such systems, and today in the industrialized, technological societies they do draw on the resources of the entire world. In this way it becomes possible for them to destroy species and ecosystems without feeling the immediate consequences, since they can turn elsewhere for support. Ecosystem people who depended on whales for their food supply would have learned not to exterminate them. Biosphere people can destroy species after species and scarcely notice their absence. Of course, earth being what it is, a reckoning can be postponed, but not avoided, and people everywhere are beginning to experience this reckoning today.

It is not possible to know when attitudes toward and relationships with wild animals began to change, but there is reason to believe that it came with the rise of domestication, the neolithic or new stone age some ten thousand years ago. Although cultivation of crops and domestication of animals does not in itself alter relationships greatly with the wild world, a growing dependence on agriculture or on domestic animals does. Since wild grazing animals do not by nature respect the boundaries between wild and tame, they would tend to go where the food was best—into the cultivated gardens; wild predators, not being fussy eaters, would as soon snap up a chicken as a quail, and would find tame sheep

Ecosystem people. The Lapp reindeer herders of Fennoscandia. Their way of life has now been eroded through contact with biosphere cultures.

easier to manage than wild deer. Once people depended for their survival on tamed species, wild species became viewed as enemies. With the rise of early civilizations, and the more total clearing of lands for irrigated agriculture, the distinction between wild and tame was more clearly marked. By then, as the ruling classes of the cities gained wealth and leisure a new relationship to the wild also developed—hunting animals for the sport and excitement of the chase. This was probably not much known in earlier times; killing was for food or other essentials, or, among the farmers, in defense of their cultivated lands. But Egyptian heiroglyphs and the tablets and bas-reliefs of Mesopotamia record game slaughters by kings and their retinue. By then also distant and dangerous gods had replaced the old nature spirits, although many of these still bore their old animal forms.

This is too brief and simple an explanation for changes that were more complex. However, as civilization spread from its Middle Eastern bases, hunting, like warfare, became more and more "the sport of kings." Peasants "poached" because they were hungry or wanted to protect their crops. In medieval times they were punished for this by loss of life or limb.

By the time of European settlement of America, wildlife in Great Britain was mostly confined to the estates of the royal family and the nobility. Title to game, if not to other animals, rested in the king, and hunting rights went with the granting of estates to aristocrats. In effect, game was under the care of the landed gentry, and its conservation or management was up to them. For the common people hunting was not generally available. The right to hunt and fish without asking permission was greatly valued by the colonists in the New World, but ownership of game remained with the crown. When independence came to the United States, game continued as the possession of the sovereign, but the sovereign now became the American state, with the government of the state gaining authority to make laws and regulations concerning game. In pioneer times this authority certainly was not exercised much; wildlife was slaughtered without thought for the future (Graham, 1947).

One could list the species that became extinct, but actually the list is not long. The passenger pigeon was the most conspicuous of these extinct species, since it had been present in the tens of millions in the forests of eastern America, and it was totally exterminated. Many other species were reduced from great abundance to scarcity. The American bison was one of the worst examples. Herds once blackened the plains and prairies—perhaps 40 million buffalo. In a brief span of years they had been killed. Their destruction was in part a military policy—wiping out the food supply of the Plains Indians—but it was also sheer unlicensed greed. Still, the bison survived on a few reserves and has now come back wherever it can be allowed to increase. But the bison was not alone; most animals that could be eaten, or had valuable furs, who competed with livestock, or who preyed on domestic animals were reduced to a level of scarcity by the end of the nineteenth century. It was this frightening reduction of wildlife, accompanied by onslaughts on the forests and rangelands that gave rise to the American conservation movement.

Conservation was to become an American movement for which the United States can take much credit. This does not imply that wildlife and other resources were not conserved and protected elsewhere, but most commonly it was a private affair of the land-owner. In America, conservation became a public movement and a concern of government, financed from the public treasury or more directly by fees charged to the user of resources. America may deserve full credit for protecting wildlife, but America must also take full blame for allowing the slaughter to continue for so long. The example was shocking to Europeans who visited this continent and it was an example followed later on the African savanna and in the Australian bush. Unfortunately, the conservation idea was slower to take hold elsewhere, but it is now having its effects.

The sequence of wildlife conservation laws in the United States has been described by Edward Graham (1947):

> The first of the game laws of the United States is usually recognized to be that passed by Connecticut in 1677. It regulated seasons and prohibited the export of game, hides, and skins. By 1700 all of the original colonies, except Georgia, had established closed seasons to protect deer. William III, through Act of the Virginia Assembly in 1699, prohibited the killing of deer from January to July, the fine for violation being 500 pounds of tobacco. In 1730 Maryland followed suit; the fine was 400 pounds of tobacco. It also prevented hunting of deer by firelight that year. The doe was first protected by Virginia in 1738, and running deer with hounds (a practice long popular in England) was prohibited by New York in 1788.

None of these provisions meant much more than an expression of good will. The killing went on. It took the better part of a century before more effective measures were taken.

During the more than two centuries of United States history, the states have guarded their authority over wildlife, even though they have been slow to exercise it. Fish and Game Commissions, the first state agencies charged with protection and restoration of game and fish, came into existence in California and New Hampshire in 1878. These first Commissions had authority but no means to exercise it except through the usual law enforcement channels. It was not until 1887 that the first states—Michigan, Wisconsin, and Minnesota—hired game wardens, specifically charged with enforcing wildlife protective legislation.

The federal government lacked authority to regulate the taking of wildlife, but nevertheless started to exercise an important role in wildlife conservation beginning with the creation of the first National Park, Yellowstone, in 1872, from which hunting was to be excluded. This was followed by others, and most recently by the establishment of 44 million acres of national parks and monuments in Alaska in 1978. The right to control the use of federal lands allowed the government to take an even more direct step toward wildlife conservation with the establishment of the first

Rocky Mountain National Park. One of a network of federal areas where wildlife is completely protected.

federal wildlife refuges on Pelican Island in Florida in 1903 and in the Wichita Mountains of Oklahoma in 1905. Like the national parks, the wildlife refuges and game ranges were to become an extensive system protecting millions of acres of land.

The treaty-making power of the federal government has enabled it to get into the wildlife regulatory field by still a different door. In 1913 a treaty was signed with Canada, Russia, and Japan protecting and managing the northern fur seal and sea otter, which were then near extinction. In 1916 a treaty was signed with Canada, and later extended to Mexico, that gave the federal government control over migratory birds—effectively removing them from direct state control. Control over the interstate movement of game was obtained through exercise of the right to regulate interstate commerce. The Lacey Act of 1900 prohibited interstate trade in game taken illegally within one state, and did much to eliminate market hunting of birds for their plumes, or other animals for their meat or hides. Gradually, federal authority has extended over species that are threatened or endangered, over marine mammals, and offshore fisheries. This has come at the expense of state authority and has been resented by those who favor local control over local resources. On the other hand, with the passage of the Federal Aid in Wildlife Restoration Act in 1937, and the Dingell-Johnson Fish Restoration Act in 1950, the federal government has aided the states in the purchase of lands for wildlife conservation and in providing funds for wildlife research.

None of these things would have happened without a growing public pressure in favor of conservation. The existence of a national belief in conservation, rather than just the action of farsighted government leaders, has brought about changes in the national outlook toward wildlife. The most recent expression of this national will has been with the development of the environmental movement of the late 1960s and early 1970s—a movement that has affected both international and national policies toward the human environment and those creatures that share the earth with the human species.

It is too early to say that the 10,000 year war on wildlife has come to an end, but certainly in the United States many of the troops have withdrawn, and those who remain are forced to fight under ever more constraining rules of warfare. In many other parts of the world the destruction goes on at an alarming rate.

3

EVERYTHING TIED TOGETHER

No living thing exists by itself. The feeling of separateness that many of us experience is in part at least an illusion. Each plant or animal or human being exists as part of a living community, some members of which live inside other species and some of which are external to each other. Each is also part of an ecosystem that includes not just living species but the nonliving environment on which each depends. Each animal must continue to breathe air, changing it as it respires, giving off a different mixture of gases than it took in. Each must take on water, passing it through the body, modifying it, storing some temporarily, giving it off again in perspiration or urine. Each depends for its existence on external temperature that must remain within a tolerable range. Each must take in food that ties it in turn to a whole range of other living species each feeding on or being fed on by other species. There is no time when any person, or animal, or plant is not in a process of interacting and interchange with all the different factors and processes of the ecosystem in which he or she is operating. I don't know how many kinds of bacteria, protozoans, or other microorganisms live normally inside a human body, but there are many. We depend on them, they depend on us. The only way to be alone on this planet is to be totally sterilized inside and out and then sealed in a lead-lined vacuum container—you can't be alone and stay alive.

A biotic community is the complex of living species that occupy a particular area and in consequence interact with one another. It can be large or small. The rainforests of the Amazon form a vast complicated biotic community; the lawn in front of a suburban house is another, small and relatively simple. Each community in turn is the living part of an ecosystem, which can be defined as a biotic community and the physical environment with which it interacts. The inescapable quality of all living species is their interrelatedness. You cannot protect or manage just one species, since what you do to it, or for it, will affect all other species it interacts with. This is the dilemma facing wildlife biologists and managers, and the full extent of it is only recently being recognized. Since all living communities and ecosystems are complex, we must learn to understand and deal with complexity. There are many simple examples that illustrate this. The cutting of trees in a forest does not just remove trees, it changes the conditions of life for all other forest species. Some increase, others disappear, and the interactions among all of them are modified. If insects of the seed-eating variety, mice, rabbits, or deer become too numerous, they can slow down or even prevent forest trees from growing back in an area, at least until they find conditions unfavorable to their own abundance and begin to decline in numbers. The destruction of "weed" species with herbicidal sprays or of insect "pests" with insecticides affects not only the target species but the entire community—from the abundant life that exists within the soil, to all the species that dwell above the ground, or those that move through the area. Often the consequences from such spraying far exceed any that were intended by the sprayer.

FUNCTIONING OF ECOSYSTEMS

The relationships within an ecological system are never static. Growth and death, change and replacement, go on continuously. Energy pours down from sunlight and is captured by green plants and transformed. Chemicals from soil, air, or water flow through the system along complicated pathways. Water moves through the system in an intricate cycle, starting from the ocean and atmosphere and returning to them again.

Energy Flow

The functioning of an ecosystem depends on an inflow of energy. This is provided by sunlight, for the most part, the energy quanta of which are captured by green plants and used in growth or metabolism, or are perhaps stored in chemical bonds in the plant starches, proteins, and other components. Animals obtain their energy from sunlight indirectly, in its transformed state, stored in chemical compounds within the plants that herbivores eat. Carnivores in turn obtain their energy, third hand, from the plant eaters. The host of parasites, decay bacteria or fungi, and other microorganisms that derive their energy from living or dead animals may be several steps farther removed from the original sunlight source.

The amount of energy available in sunlight is large in relation to the amount actually captured and used by a biotic community. Most of it is lost to the ecosystem; it is reflected back from vegetation, water, or ground surface, or radiated back as heat waves. The efficiency with which green plants transform and store the energy available to them is relatively low, often around 1 percent ends up stored in plant tissues. But efficient or not, plants are the most effective converters of solar energy into forms useful to animals and humans. Direct capture of solar energy and its use in the form of heat, electricity, or chemical compounds is becoming increasingly important to human societies, but all societies throughout time have depended on the various forms of solar power transformed into plant foods, animal tissues, or fuels derived from these sources, and this dependence will continue.

In each energy transfer, from plants, to herbivores, to carnivores, some energy is lost. No energy transfer can be 100 percent efficient. Hence, the quantity of green plant material, with its stored energy, must be large in relation to the quantity of herbivorous animals that feed on it. All the energy stored in plant carbohydrates, oils, or proteins cannot be transformed into an equal quantity of energy stored in animal tissues. Most is lost, in the form of heat, during the chemical conversions of digestion and metabolism. Similarly, the quantity of herbivore energy must be larger than the quantity of energy that ends up stored in the body of a carnivore. One pound of deer meat cannot produce one pound of mountain lion. Much is always lost in the process of conversion.

Because of the energy relationships, it is sometimes useful to portray the distribution of living organisms within an ecosystem in the form of a biotic pyramid, broad at the base and tapering toward the top. At the base are all the green plants, in the middle the herbivores, on top the carnivores—with their numbers, or total weight (biomass), tending to decrease upward from layer to layer (Fig. 3.1). However, pyramids suggest something static and permanent, and it is not the number or weight of organisms present at any one time that is important, but how much they increase in a given period through reproduction and growth. In a marine ecosystem one may find at a particular time a relatively small quantity of the floating green plants, the phytoplankton, on which most of the animal species depend. However, over a growing season that phytoplankton has the capacity to produce an enormous quantity of plant material that supports the fish and invertebrate animal populations.

In considering wildlife populations, it is sometimes true to state that predators may determine the level of prey populations, but the converse is always true. It may be, in a particular area, that the numbers of hawks, owls, weasels, and bobcats are control-

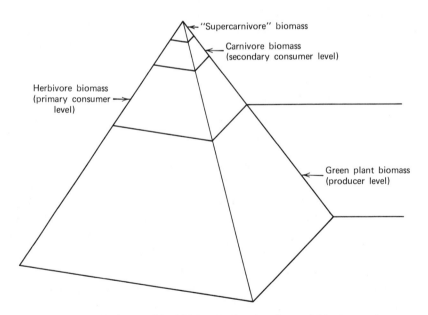

Figure 3.1. Theoretical pyramid of biomass, showing the weight of organisms supported at each trophic level of a terrestrial food chain. Similar pyramids could illustrate the number of organisms, or the calories of energy stored in each trophic level.

ling the number of quail, yet it is always the abundance and productivity of quail and other prey species that determines the level
of predators that can be supported.

Nutrient Cycling

Energy flows through an ecosystem in one direction, fueling
the physiological systems it passes through along the way, stored
for short or long periods, but ending up eventually as heat or
reflected light, too dispersed to be useful to the system. Other
pathways in an ecosystem, however, tend to be circular. Soil minerals, for example, enter green plants via the roots to be stored in
roots, stems, leaves, fruits, or seeds. Here they may be eaten by
animals and stored for a time in their tissues. When the plants or
animals die, microorganisms work on their bodies to restore the
minerals to the soil. Thus, the same molecule of a nitrate or a
phosphate may be used again and again in an ecosystem, moving
from soil to plant, to animal, back to soil, and up again over a
different pathway. Viewed over a long period of time such chemicals are in constant motion, and at any one time a high percentage
of nutrients may be tied up in plant or animal life. In some tropical forests, for example, the soils, if considered alone, are relatively
infertile. Their chemical nutrients are tied up in the trees and
animal life and are returned only briefly to the surface before
being captured once more by root systems and used by other organisms. These forest areas may seem remarkably fertile and productive, but if the forest is destroyed or removed, the soils that
once supported it can rapidly lose their fertility and are incapable
of supporting agricultural crops for very long. Without the constant turnover of minerals from the natural community, those nutrients present in the soil proper can be quickly leached away by
rain, or exhausted by being removed in the production and harvesting of a few years of farm crops. Not all tropical forest ecosystems are of this character, but a high percentage are.

Nutrients required by plants and animals are in part derived
from soil minerals obtained from the breakdown and decomposition of rocks. Some come primarily from the atmosphere, either in
rainwater, or through the action of microorganisms. Nitrogen is in
this category, with the atmosphere serving as its primary reservoir.
Some nitrogen is converted to nitrates by the action of lightning

and enters the soil through precipitation. Much of it is captured by nitrogen-fixing bacteria or algae, and may either enter the soil or be transfered to plants or animals directly from the organisms that convert it into nitrates.

Hydrologic Cycles

Water moves through an ecosystem in a different way from soil minerals (Fig. 3.2). Its principal reservoir is the ocean from which it enters the atmosphere by evaporation. Moving with the atmosphere, it enters ecosystems in the form of precipitation. This may land on trees or soil and in part be evaporated directly back to the air. What reaches the soil may sink on through and leave the ecosystem via springs, streams, or underground channels, or be stored for a time in porous rock structures. The water remaining in the soil is taken up by plant roots and may either join in chemical bonds to form plant tissues or be lost from the leaves in transpiration. Water tied up in plants is used by animals, and some desert species, for example, may get all their water in this way. Most animals will use water directly from raindrops, dew, springs,

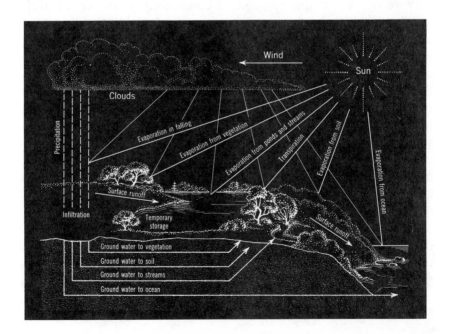

ponds, or streams. All water tied up in plant or animal tissue is in time returned to the soil or evaporated back to the atmosphere, eventually to make its way back to the oceans once again. The various pathways followed by water in the circular travels from ocean to atmosphere to land and back to ocean are termed the hydrologic cycle.

Thus, there is a constant flow of energy through an ecosystem, whereas water and chemical nutrients flow or cycle within an ecosystem. So long as input balances loss, the system remains stable. If, however, losses come to exceed input, as so often occurs through human interference, the system is modified. One community may be replaced by another, or if the loss continues for too long the ecosystem can lose its living components and totally break down.

Food Chains and Webs

The pathways over which energy and chemicals move through an ecosystem are called food chains. Normally these pathways are linked together in intricate food webs. In a simple food chain, for example, sun energy enters grass that is eaten by a meadow mouse who is eaten by a hawk. The chain has three links, each representing an energy level, or trophic level. However, such a simple chain is an abstraction or useful simplification. In nature the hawk would support various internal and external parasites, and on its death would provide food for all the organisms involved in the breakdown and decay of its tissues. Furthermore, it would be unlikely to feed only on mice, but on other species as well. The meadow mice, in turn, would be fed on also by other predators: owls, weasels, coyotes; the grass would support a variety of herbivores: leaf-sucking and leaf-mining insects, for example, which could provide food for wasps and spiders, which in turn feed flycatchers, thrushes, or other birds. Food chains always become tied into complicated webs, and actual energy pathways can be difficult to trace.

ECOSYSTEM DEVELOPMENT

A stable ecosystem does not suddenly come into existence. It may take centuries, or even thousands of years, to develop. The process by which it forms, originally, from an area that did not support life, is known as *primary biotic succession.* This, along with the slower process of organic evolution, has allowed organisms to spread over and occupy most of the surface of the earth.

Although much of the earth is now covered with vegetation, there are places where various stages of primary succession can be seen. A volcano in Italy erupts and pours molten lava down its slopes; a glacier in Alaska retreats and leaves pulverized earth and rocks in its wake; an earthquake in Chile brings to the surface bare rock from layers beneath the ground; or a lake fills in with soil and debris eroded from the surrounding lands. Each of these newly formed sites becomes an area where succession occurs. Each is eventually invaded by plant seeds or spores carried by wind, water, gravity, or animals moving from other places. Those species of plants that are hardy and able to adapt to the rigorous

Primary succession. Lichens establish themselves on a rock face, pioneering the way for the invasion of more complex vegetation.

new environment can invade and colonize the new land. They then can provide a home or food for a few kinds of animals and microorganisms. Together these will, through growth and decay, begin to break down and modify the rocky or lifeless substrate beneath them. In time they form a simple, developmental soil. Weather, sunlight, and water further modify the physical environment. As the substrate changes, as rocks break down through weathering and minerals become oxidized, other plants and animals, more exacting in their requirements, can invade and in turn bring more changes. Plant roots reach deeper and more organic debris is incorporated with the minerals of the soil. Hardy lichens may be replaced by mosses, and these in time by grasses, shrubs, or trees. Eventually a relatively stable grouping of species will occupy the area. The soils will come into balance with the climate and vegetation, become mature, and subject to only slow future change. The vegetation in turn reaches the most complex level that the combination of soil and climate can support. Animal life becomes adapted to the prevailing vegetation and in turn affects and maintains it. This end product of succession can be termed a climax ecosystem. However, it is an "end product" and stable only in a relative sense in that the process of change ceases to be obvious in terms of human lifetimes. Change continues, even if at a slow evolutionary pace. However, climax communities, barring major disturbance, tend to hold the ground, with the species of the climax replacing themselves through reproduction.

If fire, windstorm, or other disturbance should destroy a mature climax community, the process of ecosystem development that then takes place is known as secondary biotic succession. A burned-over forest regenerates itself at a much more rapid rate than that at which it was first formed through primary succession. Soils are still in place and need not be formed from a lifeless substrate. Plant seeds are usually available from nearby unburned communities, or they may survive the fire. Usually broad-leaved herbs and some grasses are the first species to become obvious; the purple fireweeds of northern forests are an example. In time these herbaceous plants will be overtopped and replaced by shrubs. Still further down the line are those trees that do best in open situations (alders, or aspens) or there may be pines that take over and shade out the shrubs to form a *subclimax* forest. Eventually, trees with seedlings that thrive in forest shade will grow up to replace the more light-demanding species. These (spruce, hemlock, beech, or maple for example) may close in to form the climax forest. Commonly—but not always—these will form a community generally similar in composition to the one that was present before the fire (Fig. 3.3).

_____The sequence that has been described is a depiction of the *dominants* at each stage of secondary succession. Often trees, shrubs, forbs, and grasses will all start growing in the first year following the fire. The herbaceous plants grow faster and dominate for a time; the shrubs then grow taller and shade them out; the trees continue to grow to overtop the smaller shrubs. The stages are not everywhere the same and they vary with substrate

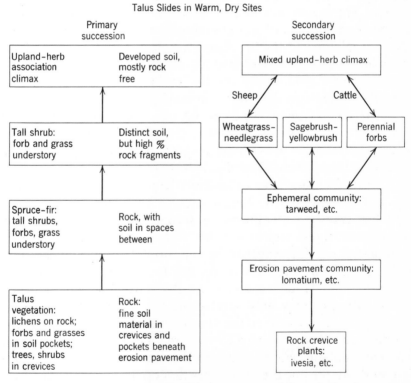

Figure 3.3. Succession in Wasatch Mountains (Ellison, 1954). *Note:* Upward arrows show normal replacements of communities in primary and secondary succession. Downward arrows show changes brought by grazing of climax community.

and the availability of seeds, or the ability of the burned-over vegetation to sprout from stumps or root crowns. Animals affect succession by carrying in seeds from other areas. They modify it by feeding on plants that develop in each successional stage. Usually, however, there is the sequence from pioneer community, through middle successional stages, to subclimax and climax communities. If disturbance is particularly severe and seed sources not readily available, a burned-over forest may remain for many decades or longer in some mid-successional stage such as chaparral or sagebrush in the western United States.

A knowledge of succession is important to the wildlife biologist or manager, since animals are as much a part of succession as plants and some species are best adapted to each stage in succession. Quail may thrive in the weeds and brush that comes in after a fire; deer and ruffed grouse will do best in middle successional stages. Few large mammals prefer a forest climax, but a variety of insectivorous birds, some seed-eating birds, shrews, and moles may do best in such vegetation. There are animal "weeds" that belong to the pioneer stages of development: white footed mice, kangaroo rats, ground squirrels. There are climax species that seem to tolerate little disturbance; the woodland caribou may be an example. Some animal populations can arrest a biotic succession as surely as it can be arrested by frequent fire. Bison, on the Great Plains of the West, maintained the short-grass prairie, where, in their absence, taller grasses would have taken over. Many types of vegetation depend on fire for their continuance, and in the absence of frequent fires become replaced by other forms; chaparral and pine savanna are examples of fire-dependent types. But fire is a normal component of their environments, as predictable as weather and climate. In order to manage wildlife, it is essential to know the relation of species to the various stages of ecosystem development, and then to maintain those stages if we wish to maintain the species. This may involve setting back succession through fire or other means; for climax species it may involve protection from disturbance.

CHANGE AND DEGRADATION

All ecosystems are subject to slow changes, but rapid change can have undesirable consequences. Degradation of an ecosystem is a change from a more productive to a less productive condition, and unless there are reasons for preferring the latter, it is undesirable.

A stable ecosystem is characterized by a constant turnover of materials, and a rough balance between losses of materials from the system and their replacement from atmosphere or substrate. Thus, in the virgin prairie, soil minerals moved upward through grass roots to leaves and stems that were fed upon by buffalo. When the buffalo died, the minerals were once more returned to the prairie soil to nourish a new generation of grass plants and buffalo. In drought years some soil would be lost to the system through wind erosion, and in other years some minerals would be leached and washed away in rainwater. But in an undisturbed prairie these losses would not be large and would be balanced in part by materials blown in by winds or carried by water from outside the system, and in part by new minerals added through the breakdown of rock fragments in the lower layers of the soil. Nitrates lost by leaching would be balanced by those fixed from the atmosphere by bacteria or algae, or by those carried in with rainwater. The prairie system was complex, with hundreds of plant species using various layers and portions of the soil, and a variety of animals feeding in turn on the various species and parts of plants or on each other. Food webs were complicated.

When Europeans first reached the prairie and attempted to live there, they found most of its components were not of direct use, and the indirect benefits were not apparent. The prairie produced buffalo, prairie chickens, and other game the settlers could eat, and there were a variety of foods that could have been used if the settlers had taken time to learn about them. But when the grasslands were plowed and planted to corn or wheat, soil nutrients, water, and sun energy were channeled directly into food production. A sparse human population, supported by the native biota, was replaced by a dense population supported by farm produce. The prairie in time became a supplier of cereal grains to the world. In the process, however, the original ecosystem was simplified, and the living components of it were largely replaced, with hundreds of species giving way to a few dominants (corn, wheat, or soybeans) and those that could live with these in the new agro-ecosystem.

Unfortunately, such tinkering with ecosystems is risky. The earth is covered with ruins of past civilizations that failed to recognize these risks in time. Soils that have developed with, and as a part of, natural vegetation may not be able to hold up when planted with one or a few species of agricultural crop plants. The original turnover of soil materials no longer takes place. Corn or wheat is harvested and taken away, and not allowed to return to the soil. Livestock fed on grain are shipped away to markets in distant cities and do not decay on the prairie. The new human masters of the land seldom allow their own remains to return to the soil. The original dense cover of prairie grasses shielded the soils from the impact of rainwater and the force of wind. Cereal grains fail to provide an adequate shielding. Thus, in the prairie region erosion began to occur, fertility began to decline, and the physical structure of the soil—formed by a dense network of plant roots—did not hold up under continual plowing and planting to cereal grains. A low point was reached in the 1930s when the Dust Bowl developed as a result of drought and continued misuse of the land. Many farmers went out of business. Those that remained began to practice a new and more expensive form of agriculture that involved adding chemical fertilizers—phosphates, potassium, and nitrates—taking up soil conservation techniques and using a variety of pesticides and herbicides to control insect pests and weeds attracted to the new kind of ecosystem created by commercial agriculture. Deterioration, however, still goes on over large areas of former prairie, as Eric Eckholm has pointed out:

Surging world grain prices in the mid-1970s, and consequent all-out production efforts by U. S. farmers in 1974 and 1975, have inculcated new fears for the land and provoked strong warnings from agricultural scientists. Government surveys show that of the nearly four million hectares of former pastures, woodlands, and idle fields converted to crops nationwide in late 1973 and early 1974, over two million hectares had inadequate conservation treatment. The average loss of topsoil to water and wind on the latter lands in 1974 was twenty-seven tons per hectares, more than double the twelve tons considered "tolerable" by government soil conservation officials (a figure still above the rate of natural soil regeneration in many regions). In the southern portion of the Great Plains, the surveys showed, the year's soil loss on twenty thousand hectares of newly planted land ranged from thirty-four to 314 tons per hectare. (Eckholm, 1976).

Mechanized, industrially based agriculture in California. Soil deterioration and erosion combined with rising energy costs threaten the future of this kind of land use.

Elsewhere in the world things are worse. In modifying ecosystems and in replacing natural vegetation, we must remain aware of the necessity for replacing the soil-forming, soil-holding qualities of that vegetation. Additional problems also arise from the simplification of ecosystems. When the original variety of vegetation and animal life is replaced by a few cultivated species, an ideal, uniform habitat is created for those species that feed on cultivated plants. Lacking natural predators or other enemies, such species can increase to great numbers. The use of pesticides can bring temporary relief, but most commercial organic pesticides now in use are nonselective, killing friend and foe alike, and further reduce populations of natural predators. Furthermore, through killing off individuals most vulnerable to the particular poison, these tend to select for insecticide-resistant forms of the crop-destroying insect, causing a continued search for new or stronger pesticides. These in turn have serious side-effects, which often are their principal effects, that destroy wild animal life.

In most instances, lands that are damaged by unwise attempts to make them grow unsuitable crops or by attempts to produce or support too many domestic animals can be repaired. Sometimes simple rest is all that is needed, allowing natural processes of biotic succession to put things back together again. Sometimes more drastic measures are called for: erosion control devices, fertilization, replanting with species that can restore structure and fertility to the soil. Some lands have been pushed too far. A point of no return is reached when the rate of erosion or extent of soil destruction is too far advanced to allow recovery within a calculable period of time. Some of the Western ranges, grazed too heavily for too long, have reached this point. Mountain slopes are particularly vulnerable because once the soil has washed downhill, it cannot ordinarily be put back in place; the bare bones of the mountains begin to show—scenic perhaps, but not productive.

Most severe wildlife problems are associated with lands that have in one way or another been misused. Although some species occasionally increase to spectacular levels in relatively undisturbed ecosystems, such increases of previously benign species of wildlife to levels at which they become serious pests are a symptom of land misuse.

DISTRIBUTION OF BIOTIC COMMUNITIES

Although the general principles that govern the functioning of ecosystems and determine the place of wildlife within them are the same all over the world, the kinds of ecosystems vary greatly. There are many ways for classifying, describing, and mapping those ecosystems on the basis of the natural communities they support. Here, for simplicity, I will consider only two: one that emphasizes the differences in animal life in various parts of the world, the other that stresses the similarities of biotic communities that occur in similar climatic and physiographic regions. These two will be blended into a single system, that combines the best features of both.

Faunal Regions

One of the earlier efforts to map and describe the distribution of biota was that of P. L. Sclater who in 1858 classified the natural regions of the world on the basis of their bird faunas. His system was further developed on the basis of other animal species by Alfred Russel Wallace.

In the time of Sclater and Wallace the world was first becoming well known and accurately described. Wallace recognized that animal distribution was characterized by marked differences between regions whose boundaries were sometimes well defined, but more often blended gradually between adjoining regions. The boundaries did not necessarily coincide with the edges of continents; thus North America and northern Eurasia were more similar than northern and southern Asia. Each of Wallace's regions

Elephants, lions, leopards, rhinos, and great apes occur in both the African and Oriental biogeographical regions.

represented a center of origin for many of the species that lived there. Similarities between regions resulted from interchange of species between them, over land bridges or other pathways, and frequently reflected the amount of continental drift that had taken place, separating lands that were once joined together. Major differences between regions reflected long periods of isolation. Australia, cut off from the rest of the world by ocean barriers over millions of years, is the most distinctive in its fauna. Its native mammals consist mostly of marsupials—kangaroos, wallabies, possums and their relatives—or monotremes—the echidna and platypus. The Oriental and African regions have many similarities, including the presence in both of lions, leopards, elephants, rhinos, and great apes. However, they have been separate for long enough so that each of these groups is represented by different species. The Neotropical and Nearctic regions have many differences, caused by isolation during most of the period when mammalian evolution was taking place, but also similarities resulting from the spread of species from one area into the other over the Panama isthmus, a land bridge established in Pleistocene times. The tapir and peccaries have moved northward over this bridge; North American deer and mountain lion have moved southward into the Neotropics.

Wallace's faunal regions have been modified by Udvardy (1975), and his classification is presented in Table 3.1. It does not differ greatly from Wallace's original breakdown, but also takes into account the distribution of plant life as well as animals.

Biomes

Although each faunal region differs in the species of animals and plants present, there are nevertheless strong similarities among the major ecosystems occurring within them. Thus, the general character and arrangement of the vegetation, which reflects climate and substrate, is markedly similar in the humid tropics of the Oriental, African, Australian, and Neotropical regions. All have rain forests that are similar in appearance. There is little also to distinguish the forests of northern Siberia in general appearance from those in northern Canada. The species of trees may

Table 3.1   Biogeographic Realms (Udvardy, 1975)

Realm	Wallace's Terminology	Area Included
Palaearctic	Palaearctic	Northern Asia, Europe and Mediterranean Africa
Nearctic	Nearctic	Northern North America (approx. to central Mexico)
Africotropical	Ethiopian	Sub-Saharan Africa
Indomalayan	Oriental	Indian subcontinent and southeast Asia through to Celebes and Sunda islands
Oceanian	—	Islands of South Pacific westward through New Guinea
Australian	Australian	Australia and Tasmania
Antarctic	—	Antarctica, sub-Antarctic islands, and New Zealand
Neotropical	Neotropical	Latin America, north approx. to central Mexico including West Indies

differ, but their form is the same, and the ways in which plants are grouped into communities are similar. It is therefore possible to describe certain large biotic communities, or biomes, that occur in all faunal regions with similar climates. Within each of these the wildlife is also of a similar character. For example, the tropical forests of Africa support leopards; those of South America, jaguars. The two cats are not close relatives, but in appearance and ways of life they resemble one another.

The principal types of biomes in the world are:

Tundra—low vegetation of polar and subpolar regions

Forest—tree vegetation, continuous or nearly so, characteristic of moist temperate and tropical regions

Deserts—low vegetation with shrubs of intermediate height characteristic of arid temperate and tropical areas

Grasslands—low vegetation characteristic of climates intermediate between forest and desert.

These can all be further subdivided. For our purposes we should at least note different categories of forests:

Taiga, or northern coniferous forest: of the subarctic and high mountain chains.

Temperate, broadleaved, deciduous forests: of areas with warm, wet summers and snowy, cold winters.

Tropical and subtropical humid forests (rain forests and their relatives): of humid tropical and subtropical areas without a prolonged dry season.

Tropical and subtropical deciduous forests and woodlands (monsoon and thorn forests and their relatives): of tropical or subtropical areas with pronounced dry seasons.

Mediterranean forest, woodland, and scrub: of temperate areas with dry summers and cool winters (California chaparral, Mediterranean maquis and garrigue, South African fynbosch).

The term woodland, as used here, implies an open forest, often with trees lower than in a true forest. Through burning or other causes this can be opened into *savanna,* in which trees are widely spaced, individually or in groves, in an area that is predominantly grassland. Typically, savannas occupy a zone between forests and grasslands.

Biotic provinces (Biogeographical provinces)

Following the example of Lee Dice (1943) and others in an attempt to find a single system of classification useful for species conservation, I tried in 1972 and later to combine the concept of faunal and floral regions, characterized by marked taxonomic differences, and the biome system. A working system of classification for the natural regions of the world was developed and further improved by Udvardy (1975). The result is a system of biotic provinces that differ from each other in either the species of animals and plants that occur within them or show marked differences in vegetation. The biotic provinces for North America—the Nearctic portion of it—are shown in Table 3.2 and Figure 3.4. These are

Table 3.2   Biogeographic Provinces of Nearctic North America (Udvardy, 1975)

1. Sitkan	12. Aleutian Islands
2. Oregonian	13. Alaskan tundra
3. Yukon taiga	14. Canadian tundra
4. Canadian taiga	15. Arctic archipelago
5. Eastern forest	16. Greenland tundra
6. Austroriparian	17. Arctic desert and icecap
7. Californian	18. Grasslands
8. Sonoran	19. Rocky Mountains
9. Chihuahuan	20. Sierra-Cascade
10. Tamaulipan	21. Madrean-Cordilleran
11. Great Basin	22. Great Lakes

Numbers refer to areas indicated on Figure 3.4.

broad subdivisions, reflecting major biotic differences. To be useful locally they require further breakdown into biotic districts—a task which, for most provinces, remains to be done.

ECOLOGIC NICHES

Each biome has animals that may have evolved separately from different genetic stocks but play similar roles or have the same function, whether the biome is located in Africa or North America. There are a certain number of ecologic niches, or places in the environment suited to animals in each biome. In the course of evolution, species evolve to occupy a particular niche. Where niches are similar, species of similar function will evolve even in widely separate areas. Thus, the grasslands of Australia include a variety of niches for grazing animals of various sizes. Although no ungulates were present in Australia to fill these niches, the native marsupial stock has given rise to large grazing kangaroos, smaller wallabies, wombats, and other smaller herbivores suited to occupy the grassland biome. A niche similar to that of the kangaroo may be occupied in America by the pronghorn, in Eurasia and Africa by different gazelles, and in South America by the guanaco, representing three different families of mammals. The presence of these

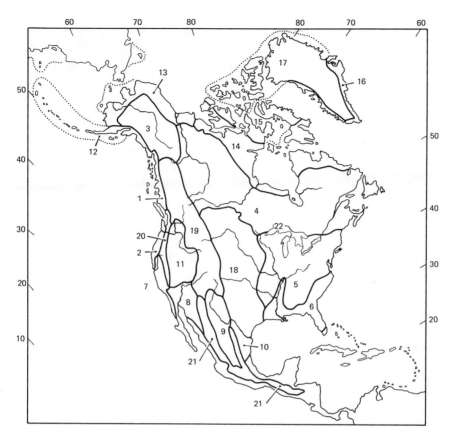

Figure 3.4. Biogeographical provinces of the nearctic biogeographical realm (M.D.F. Udvardy, 1975).

herbivores, in turn, helps create a niche for a dog-like carnivore: the dingo in Australia, the coyote and wolf in North America, the jackel and hunting dog in Africa. Some of these come from different ancestral stocks.

This concept of ecologic niche is useful for considering similarities between biomes where similar habitats tend to be occupied by species similar in function, though not necessarily in appearance. But the idea of ecologic niche merits further consideration. Grinnell (1943) has used the term to mean the distributional area within which a species is held by its structural or behavioral limitations. Thus, in a grassland region there are many niches for birds. A species such as the meadowlark is adapted only to grasslands or similar areas of low cover. Within the grassland, however, it prefers certain types of cover and feeds on certain sizes and categories of food. No other species in the region prefers precisely the same food or cover. Consequently, each species has exclusive occupancy of its own niche, although portions of it may be used by other birds and mammals. If another species attempted to use the same niche entirely, to seek the same cover and eat the same foods, it would compete directly with the meadowlark. Either the meadowlark would be displaced by its competitor, or the competitor could not become established (Gause, 1934).

However, there are other ways of looking at this situation. It can be argued that a species and its niche tend to evolve together. Bison occupying a grassland create the kind of grassland most favorable to bison, and thus create a bison niche. A tule elk occupying a grassland modifies it in other ways and creates a tule-elk niche. When cattle are introduced to either area, the cattle can fit into the bison niche without changing it too greatly. In the tule elk–grassland niche, the cattle have a totally different effect, modifying the grassland greatly, from bunchgrass prairie to annual grass range.

The concept that each biome has similar niches and that these will be occupied in different biotic provinces by species of similar function and often of similar appearance is only partially true. For similar species to evolve takes time, and in some regions insufficient time has been available. Thus, the African grasslands support a great variety of grazing ungulates, and the North American grasslands few. There is no reason to believe the American grasslands do not have more niches than there are ungulates to fill them. In fact, in the Ice Ages, North America once supported a much greater variety of grazers and browsers. We can only assume that not enough time has been available in America for new species to evolve to take the place of those that became extinct during Pleistocene and post-Pleistocene times. African mammals, spared many of the rigors of the Ice Ages, did not lose so much of their original Pleistocene variety. To test this idea, we could move African (or Eurasian) mammals to North America.

This has been done. The horse, introduced in the sixteenth century, spread rapidly through the grasslands of North and South America; the burro adapted readily to the American arid lands. In New Mexico and Texas a number of African species have been introduced and have apparently fitted in with little difficulty. There is danger, of course, in such introduction of exotics, since their niches may overlap those of native species and lead to their disappearance. This has in fact happened too often, in too many areas.

The idea that each species has its own niche and no two species can occupy the same niche in the same area is useful for understanding the way species have sorted themselves out over time in well-established natural communities. However, it does cause one to lose sight of the dynamics of species interactions and of events that take place in disturbed communities. For example, what I have termed the tule elk–grassland niche has disappeared from the California Central Valley and, despite the tendency for ecosystems to reform and regroup following disturbance through the process of biotic succession, the old tule elk–grassland niche will never be reformed in quite the same way that it was. The elk survives, and most of the grassland plant species survive, but the space taken over by exotic species probably will not ever again be entirely relinquished. There is a niche for tule elk in the new grasslands, but it is not the same niche. However, neither is it the same elk. The present stock has evolved from a few survivors out of tens of thousands of elk that were once in California. How it differs genetically from its forebears is not known, but it could be markedly different in many physiological and behavioral ways.

Off the coast of California there was once a niche for the Pacific sardine, a small plankton-feeding fish that travelled in enormous schools. The sardine population was greatly reduced and eliminated over parts of its range by heavy fishing pressure in combination with oceanographic changes. The fishing pressure has been relieved, but the sardine has not recovered. It appears that the northern anchovy, a similar plankton feeder, has moved in to take over its niche. If the anchovies were knocked out, would the sardine come back? We don't know.

In the Antarctic, the blue whale occupied a niche in which it depended on krill—a small shrimp-like crustacean—for its principal food. When its numbers were reduced to near extinction by heavy whaling pressure, its niche may also have been reduced. Certainly there has been an enormous increase in another krill-feeder—the crab-eating seal—possibly a considerable increase in the smaller minke whales, and in various krill-eating sea birds. The blue whale has not bounced back once whaling pressure was relieved. We do not know if it will ever come back. If massive human exploitation of the Antarctic krill fishery takes place, it is highly unlikely that there will be space for blue whales also.

4

A PLACE TO LIVE

If we want to maintain or restore animals, we must be prepared to leave them a place to live. That place to live is what we mean by habitat: a space and an environment suited to a particular species. Some species don't tolerate disturbance by humans. For them to exist we have to leave their land alone. Most species did very well before humans appeared on the scene, but nevertheless seem to benefit from those activities that have created a more favorable habitat for them. Some species seem to require human presence, and these are often species we don't particularly care for—for example, Norway rats or house mice. However, we support them by our activities and thus one could say we deserve them. Habitat management to benefit wildlife can mean anything from complete protection of remote areas to drastic disturbance of vegetation to create those successional stages favorable to certain species. It has been said by Aldo Leopold that the recreational value of a wild animal is inversely proportional to the amount of "management" expended on it. However, he used the word to mean effort expended to change or maintain a particular habitat. In all habitats there is a limit to the number of animals of any one species that can be supported. That limit is known as the carrying capacity of the habitat.

It is possible to confuse habitat with ecologic niche. One has been described as the animal's "address" and the other as its "profession." The two terms are not that easily separated, since the animal's "profession" is carried out only at a particular "address." The habitat for a meadow mouse may be a meadow, but the mouse uses it in a particular way, creating a niche within it that does not necessarily involve all the components of the meadow environment. The meadow may be a habitat for a hundred species, but the meadow mouse niche within it is fully occupied only by meadow mice. There are only a certain number of spaces for meadow mice in a particular meadow, and when these are filled, the carrying capacity for meadow mice has been reached. There may still be space for other species that use the meadow differently—badgers, pocket gophers, jackrabbits, for example.

The term habitat is sometimes also confused with the geographic range of a species. Geographic range is a broader term indicating the map area in which a species occurs. But one expects to find a particular species only in suitable habitats within a geographic range. The particular range of a species is determined generally by climate, vegetation, and topography to which the species can become adapted. Often a species is capable of living within a much broader geographic range than it actually occupies. Its place of origin, ability to travel, or the presence of barriers that it is unable to cross may result in its occupying a much smaller space that it has the potential to occupy. Human occupancy of the earth has changed the ranges of many species, expanding some and contracting others. At the same time, species themselves are not fixed entities, but are evolving and changing, developing the capacity to occupy environments differing from those used in the past. All species tend to press on the boundaries of their geographic ranges, sending colonists to occupy new areas as the carrying capacities of their original habitats are exceeded.

The question "What determines carrying capacity?" is not as easy to answer as it might seem. Certain obvious factors are involved: the right kind of food, and the quantity of it available; the presence of water, for most animals; the right kind of soil, for some species; the necessary topography—mountains, plains, lakes, streams; and that general term known as cover, meaning arrangements of land and vegetation suited to nesting, resting, hiding, flying, and all the various activities the species performs. But we cannot know all the factors, even for the human species.

ENOUGH TO EAT

Vertebrates, in contrast to less complicated animals, have complex nutritional needs. Basic to all is the need for energy required to keep warm, to move, to circulate blood, to transform chemicals from one form to another, and to carry out all the work that is done inside the animal's body or that the body itself does as a unit. Energy flows through the animal's body in a one-way direction. It can be stored temporarily, but new supplies must be available at frequent intervals. Energy is provided most abundantly by the carbohydrates (starches and related substances) in plants, which are broken down into sugars in the process of digestion. The sugars in turn are broken down (oxidized) to yield Calories of heat energy. (Calories, in nutritional terms of kilogram calories, are the amount of heat needed to raise the temperature of 1 kilogram of water one degree Celsius.) Human caloric needs are roughly 2,000 to 3,000 Calories per day. A deer may require 6,000 to 10,000 Calories per day for growth and development, depending on its size. Caloric needs are very high for some smaller animals—hummingbirds and shrews, for example. Shrews, held overnight in a live trap, will frequently starve to death before morning. Fats can be substituted for carbohydrates, and proteins can also be an energy source, but starches are more efficiently handled by most herbivores and omnivores.

In addition to energy needs, vertebrates have specific nutritional requirements. Some fatty acids are essential to the diet, and are supplied by fats or oils. A number of vitamins are required to provide the enzymes needed for metabolic processes. Many different chemical elements, collectively termed macronutrients, are needed in large quantity. Calcium and phosphorus are examples. Other elements—the micronutrients—are needed in minute quantities (trace elements), and too large an amount can be poisonous. Copper and cobalt exemplify this type. All animals must have nitrogen, in the form of many different amino acids, all of which are essential to nutrition. These amino acids, the components of plant proteins, form the building blocks for animal proteins. A satisfactory food for growth, maintenance, and reproduction must provide all these essentials in proper quantity and in an adequate balance.

Carnivores have developed a simple answer to nutritional needs. By eating other animals they find their dietary needs neatly packaged and easily digestible. Rarely do they suffer from deficiencies in food quality. When food becomes limiting, it is usually quantity that is lacking. Among herbivores, the seed eaters most closely approach carnivores in their dietary relationships. A plant stores sufficient food in its seeds to provide for the initial requirements of the new plant. This is often done at the expense of essential materials within the parent plant, which has its food reserves depleted after producing seeds. Seed-eating animals are likely to obtain most of their dietary needs within a seed, and quantity rather than quality is the most likely food deficiency.

Seed eaters, in general, are less likely to be destructive to their habitat than are other herbivores. Plants produce seeds in far greater amounts than are needed for replacement of the parents. Animals can feed on the surplus. Admittedly, concentrations of seed eaters, temporarily gathered, can devastate farm crops and may damage wild plant reproduction. Usually however, seed eaters are unlikely to destroy their habitat. When seeds are scarce or seed crops fail they starve, much as a carnivore starves when its prey is absent.

Other herbivores, the grazers and browsers, are little affected by food lack in a quantitative sense, except in barren or badly overgrazed areas. Usually they can obtain enough plant material to fill their stomachs, but frequently they suffer from deficiencies in food quality. If their numbers are low in relation to production of plant food, they have few nutritional problems. If they can select for species of plant, and feed on buds, new leaves, and terminal shoots of shrubs or trees, they can obtain a diet high in essential protein, minerals, and other requirements. However, if forced to feed on less desirable species or older plant parts, qualitative nutritional troubles may develop. In a single area, one species of shrub will contain 16 percent protein in its terminal twigs, whereas another, at the same time of year, will have only 3 to 4 percent. Within a single species a favorably situated plant may have 14 percent protein, and another, less well located, will have less than 7 percent. If few animals are browsing they can select for better quality. Too many animals may end up with full stomachs, but serious malnutrition.

Effects on Plants

If browsers can feed on the annual growth of plants without cutting into the necessary reserves for plant maintenance and growth (metabolic reserve), their numbers can be considered in good balance with their habitat. If, however, they begin to crop the metabolic reserve of a plant they may injure it and eventually kill it (W. Dasmann, 1945). Certain shrubs and trees show an ability to withstand heavy browsing without damage. Others are highly sensitive. Thus, Aldous (1952), in a study carried out in Minnesota, found that 100 percent of the annual twig growth could be removed each winter from willow or mountain maple without injuring the plant. In fact, growth was stimulated by this degree of cropping. However, northern white cedar and some broad-leaved shrubs could stand no more than light use (20 percent or less of the annual twig growth) without injury. Repeated heavy use weakened or killed the plant.

Where trees have grown above the reach of browsing animals, a heavy population of browsers sometimes will remove all the plant parts within reach, thus creating a *browse line* in the forest or thicket. This usually does not harm the tree, but will affect future populations of animals that attempt to use the area. Some shrubs, when heavily cropped, develop a basket-like hedged shape. When this happens, the inner branches within the basket are protected from use by the dense network of outside twigs. Such shrubs are less likely to be damaged by overuse than shrubs that fail to develop this protective form.

Grazers, like browsers thrive as long as they can feed on the tender young shoots, buds, and leaves of grasses and forbs, but may encounter nutritional difficulties when forced to eat old, coarse leafage. Unlike most browsers, they can destroy their food supply in a single season of use, eating plants back to the crown and sometimes pulling them out, roots and all. This can occur where domestic livestock are forced to concentrate on limited areas, but rarely takes place in the wild. It would not occur in any reasonably stocked area, since grazers prefer not to feed this closely. Grasses and forbs, like woody plants, vary in nutritional value and palatability. Grazers eat the more palatable species first, thus removing competition with the less palatable forms. Continued heavy grazing can thus shift a grassland from a mixture of useful forage plants to a largely unpalatable assemblage of weeds.

Dietary Needs

Although birds and mammals have similar nutritional requirements, all species do not have the same dietary requirements. Some must find all the necessary elements for nutrition ready-made in the plants on which they feed. Others support an internal flora and fauna of bacteria and protozoa in their digestive tracts that can synthesize many of the animal's requirements from relatively simple raw materials. The normal mammalian digestive tract can break down plant proteins into amino acids that then pass into the blood stream. No mammal can synthesize these amino acids; they must be in final form. Ruminants, however, get around this problem by carrying in one of the four chambers of their stomach, the rumen or paunch, a favorable environment in which bacteria can thrive. These bacteria are capable of synthesizing amino acids from simple nitrogenous sources, so that a ruminant may not require complex proteins in its diet. Ruminants have been supported experimentally on a diet of urea and cellophane, with the urea supplying the nitrogen from which bacteria build amino acids and the cellophane providing the carbohydrate that the bacteria break down into digestible sugars. Rumen bacteria can also synthesize many of the needed vitamins—Vitamin A is an exception—if the chemical raw materials are available. A ruminant is thus equipped to survive on foods lacking in many components that another mammal would need to find in its diet. Some nonruminants support a similar group of bacteria in the caecum.

Seasonal Changes in Food Values

A complete study of the nutritional value of any food is laborious and has not been done for most wild plants. Various measures of nutritional value, however, have been made. Commonly the dry-weight percentage of protein is used as an index to nutritional quality. There is no guarantee, however, that a plant high in protein will have enough of all other essential elements, but commonly this measurement does seem to work.

The nutritional value of plants follows an annual cycle in the temperate zone. During the early growing season of spring, nutritional values will be high, and protein content reaches a maximum. After flowering and seed production, the protein content of the twigs and leaves falls off. When the plant dries out or becomes dormant, protein reaches a low point. In Figure 4.1 the seasonal

California chaparral. The production of highly nutritious forage for deer and other wildlife varies with the fire history of this vegetation.

change in protein for deer food plants growing in the chaparral
region of California is shown. It will be noted that old-growth
chamise, one of the common species of deer foods, reaches a protein peak in April-June and falls off sharply in protein as the dry
summer season progresses. Browsing may stimulate some sprout
growth and an increase in protein during the summer, but a low
point is reached in the autumn months. Following the first fall
rains some additional sprouting may occur, until winter cold
brings on further dormancy. Protein values, however, remain
higher in the usually mild winters than in the late fall. Starting in
February, temperatures rise while soil moisture remains high, encouraging growth. Protein then increases as shrubs send out new
leaves and shoots.

Since a level of at least 13 percent protein, dry weight, is
needed for optimal growth and reproduction in deer, a deer forced
to feed entirely on old chamise growth would not receive an adequate diet. Even the level of 9.5 percent protein needed for moderate growth is not achieved, and the 7 percent level required for

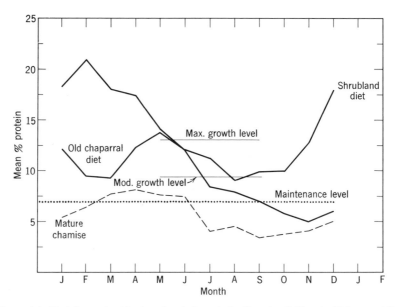

Figure 4.1. Protein content in deer foods from Lake County, California (Taber and Dasmann, 1958).

body maintenance is only reached in April. Since a deer would not confine itself to a diet of chamise, but would seek other shrubs of higher food value as well as herbaceous plants, the diet obtained in an old-growth area of chaparral would have the protein content illustrated in Figure 4.1. This would not fall below the maintenance level except in late fall and winter, but would only approach the optimal level during a brief period in the spring. Deer can survive on this diet, but not thrive. In managed areas of shrubland, where a mixture of brush and grass occurs, deer are better situated. Protein levels are above 13 percent for six months in the year and do not fall below the 7 percent level. Deer living in this habitat are more productive than in other areas. Nowhere in this chaparral region, however, do deer reach a large size, develop massive antlers, or mature early. Thus, their diet, restricted by the competition of numbers, rarely reaches an optimum.

Soils and Nutrition

A general relationship between soil fertility, food quality, and the abundance, size, health, and vigor of wild animals has long been known. Soils that have a proper balance of those minerals needed for adequate nutrition will support more wild animal life than soils that are deficient in any element. Unfortunately, the best and most fertile soils have to a large degree been taken over for the production of farm crops and are no longer available for wildlife production. Most animals must live on the less productive soils—a factor that has contributed to the decline in wildlife abundance. The tendency for animals to seek more nutritious foods often leads them into conflict with farmers.

Soils in the chaparral region of California are generally shallow, low in water-holding capacity, and not highly fertile. When deer from this region have access to food grown on more fertile alluvial soils, they grow to larger size, have larger antlers, and mature faster. Deer placed in pens and fed on an optimum diet can reach a larger size in their first year than some adults in the wild can attain in a lifetime. William Longhurst, working at Hopland, California, with deer from local stocks, has produced fawns that grow larger than wild yearlings, and yearlings that exceed the weight of many adult deer raised on foods grown on wild-land soils of the region. His results confirm the studies of Wood and others in British Columbia (1962), and those of French and others in Pennsylvania (1956). In the Pennsylvania study, white-tailed deer yearlings weighing up to 180 pounds were reared on carefully balanced diets. These animals developed four-point antlers at an age when most wild deer would have only small spikes. The failure of most deer, even on well-managed wild lands, to develop the size and vigor of these animals suggests deficiencies in the fertility of wild-land soils.

Other Factors Affecting Food Supply

Since climates change over long cycles and weather varies from year to year, food production and quality also fluctuate. Prolonged droughts in the Great Plains such as those recorded in the 1930s and 1950s directly affected the food produced and the biomass of animal life that could be supported. Under drought conditions there was also a change from tall prairie grasses with higher moisture requirements to shorter, more drought-resistant forms. Species requiring tall grass lost their habitat, whereas those thriving in lower or less dense vegetation were favored. Dry years in desert areas can mean no rainfall at all and no food production. Desert species have to depend on reserves left from previous years, and only the more favorably situated animals survive. Wet years in the desert favor phenomenal food production, and allow for great increases in animal numbers.

Disturbance of mature vegetation through fire or other kinds of clearing also has a marked effect on food supplies. Those species requiring foods produced only in more mature vegetation—tree fruits and seeds, for examples—must move out of the burned area or die. Those favored by the successional growth that follows disturbance will increase. Where minerals needed for protein production are in relatively short supply in the soils, the release of minerals previously bound up in living plants and their restoration to the soil in the form of ash, following a fire, usually leads to marked gains in protein content of the plants that grow up in the burned area (Fig. 4.2).

Perhaps throughout human history people have attempted to encourage wild animals, of certain preferred species, by providing them with food. Backyard feeders and bird baths are common in suburban gardens, and bird seed is a popular item in food stores.

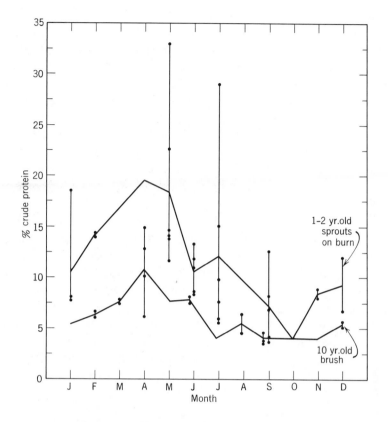

Figure 4.2. Protein content of chamise in response to burning. (Vertical lines show range of values from individual plants.) (Taber and Dasmann, 1958.)

In less enlightened days national park rangers used to encourage bears and other wild animals to come out and be seen by feeding them at garbage dumps. Such efforts can increase wildlife populations, but create dependent populations, which in time lose their fear of human beings. A tame song bird can be nice to have around, but a fearless grizzly bear is likely to cause problems. Artificial feeding of game animals to increase their numbers and provide more "trophy size" heads has long been practiced in intensively managed hunting reserves in Europe. However, once such a program is instituted, a dependent population of animals unable to maintain themselves on natural food supplies will be created. Such a population, if kept at an artificially high level, can be destructive to those natural food plants that are available, further reducing the carrying capacity of the natural vegetation (Woolf and Harder, 1979). They must then be intensively managed, and their numbers kept in check by heavy hunting, or they will die off, perhaps to levels lower than existed before the feeding program was instituted.

More desirable and lasting results can be obtained by improving natural food supplies, rather than providing hay, grain, or other supplements. Use of fire to induce successional growth, mechanical clearing to remove undesirable plants, reseeding or transplanting useful food plants are all techniques that can be used to enhance food supplies on a more permanent basis. However, before one starts on such activities one must be certain that an actual increase in wildlife numbers is desirable, and understand what will happen to the surplus produced. Wildlife populations increase to the carrying capacity of their habitats, and when this capacity is reached, excess numbers may die off. Increasing carrying capacities can increase wildlife numbers, but this could only lead eventually to bigger and more spectacular die-offs. Furthermore, efforts to increase food can be nonproductive if it turns out that some other factor needed by the animal is in short supply.

COVER

The term cover is used in several senses that can cause confusion. In one usage it is *shelter* from weather—a place to get in out of the sun and wind, or conversely a place to lie or stand in the sun or wind. This may be provided by the arrangement of vegetation, or by the ground itself, as when a den is dug into the earth or an animal seeks shelter on a cliff face or a deep valley. A second usage is *escape cover,* which can be a dense tangle of vegetation into which predators cannot easily follow, or steep ground, or a rock face. This could also include *roosting cover,* a place where birds rest at night where they can be less vulnerable to predators. *Nesting cover* is still another category, a place where the vegetation is or can be arranged into suitable shelter for a nest. The presence or absence of any of these kinds of cover can increase or reduce the carrying capacity of an area, although in the case of escape cover the carrying capacity would only be affected if predators have a limiting influence. (The term *covert* is sometimes used in the same sense as cover.)

The habitat requirements of a species usually involve several different arrangements of vegetation. A sage grouse needs bare open areas for strutting grounds, used during courtship periods, but more usually seeks extensive stands of sagebrush for feeding. A ruffed grouse thrives best in an area of young hardwood trees and brush with some herbaceous vegetation, during most seasons, but in winter will depend on a conifer swamp for shelter. A blue grouse in winter will remain for long periods in a dense fir or spruce tree, feeding on the buds and being sheltered from storms by the snow-covered branches. A mule deer in winter will feed in a sagebrush flat, but during storms seeks groves of junipers or pinyon pine. For escape cover a quail uses a dense brush patch or pile of brush, through which it can dodge and run to lose a following hawk, and a grove of trees, on which it can roost to escape ground-hunting carnivores. Human hunting affects cover requirements. Animals that at other times are found in open ground may seek deep shelter during hunting season, but those species that depend on sight and speed to locate and escape from enemies may seek the most open areas when subject to hunting. This has been a factor in the decline of many desert and plains animals, since motorized hunters can travel faster than any antelope, kangaroo, ostrich or emu can run.

Cover is subject to an annual cycle as plants grow or become dormant. A suitable area for summer shelter or escape can lose its value when leaves are shed in the autumn. A dense grassland, useful for shelter in spring, becomes too open as the grasses dry in the autumn. Severe weather not only increases the need for cover, but can also destroy it. Hurricanes in the Gulf region, or other severe wind storms, can eliminate roosting or nesting trees and thus reduce bird populations, even though the individual birds may escape the storms.

For cover improvement, vegetation change through burning, mechanical clearing, or planting is usually practiced. However, artificial devices can also be valuable, since most wild animals seem to be devoid of aesthetic sensibilities. Dead brush is piled up in oak savannas to provide escape cover for quail and thus increase the carrying capacities of areas where food and other needs are sufficiently supplied. A line of telephone poles across a grass-land creates an artificial savanna for flycatchers, hawks, or owls that like to launch their hunting forays from a high perch. Defunct motor vehicles have been piled in shallow coastal waters to create artificial reefs that serve as shelter for a variety of fish. Oil-drilling platforms seem as useful to cormorants for resting and sunning as would natural rocks. However, people do have aesthetic criteria, and many devices that animals would find satisfactory can ruin the scene for human observers.

Improving cover arrangements for wildlife involves consideration of all the habitat requirements of a species. To be useful, the various cover requirements must be met within convenient distances from food sources and water supplies.

WATER

All animals require water, but species vary greatly in their need for drinking water. The kangaroo rat can live on dry seeds in desert areas and will not drink water. It has evolved to suit this environment through changes in kidney function that cut down on water loss from excretion; by an ability to obtain water through the metabolism of starch; and by becoming largely nocturnal in habit, avoiding the desiccating heat of the day in underground burrows. Many other desert species have developed adaptations that permit survival without free water through an evolved ability to obtain water from their food. Among large animals, the oryx and addax antelopes of the Sahara do not drink, and both the eland and springbuck can exist in waterless areas of the Kalahari. Many species will go without drinking when vegetation is green and succulent, but turn to water supplies when the vegetation becomes drier.

When a species requires drinking water, its home area must include a permanent water supply, or it must develop a pattern of migrating to water during the dry season. Areas too far from water will not be utilized even if food and cover are abundant. Animals occupying areas in which water sources are some distance apart may develop patterns of movement that result in their occupying larger tracts of ground than animals of the same species will in areas where water is plentiful. However, for an area to be used,

Waterholes are key to species distribution and abundance in dry regions.

water must be available at distances related to the animal's speed of travel and its water needs. Species that need to drink only once in several days can use areas farther from water than those that drink daily. Birds that can fly quickly over long distances can use areas far from water supplies.

The carrying capacity of an area for species that require drinking water can be limited by the distribution of water points. Any single water source, regardless of the amount of water present, will support only a limited number of animals. The actual limitation will often be imposed by the food supply within the area near water. To increase the carrying capacity of an area, more watering points could be developed, thus making available food sources that otherwise would not be utilized.

Water development has become a technique frequently used

in wildlife management. In the American West, wildlife has been increased by the use of such devices as the "gallinaceous guzzler" developed by Ben Glading of the California Department of Fish and Game. This collects water during the rainy season on a concrete or plastic apron and holds it in underground storage, where it can be reached during the dry season by quail and other game birds. Big game "guzzlers" are also used for desert bighorn, mule deer, and other large mammals. However, water development for animals is risky. Since animal numbers are always greater near water supplies than they are far from them, serious habitat damage can be done around water holes if there is no means for controlling animal numbers. Increasing the number of watering points does serve to temporarily alleviate the damage by spreading out the use, but in the long run serves to extend the damage, as populations increase to the carrying capacity provided by means of the new water sources. In arid lands, the damage done to vegetation by excessive animal numbers around water holes can be virtually permanent since rates of recovery are slow at best.

Aquatic and semi-aquatic wildlife present a different array of habitat needs from those of upland and arid areas. Confined to water or areas immediately nearby, their numbers are limited by the distribution of lakes, ponds, streams, and marshes. These wet areas have been particularly hard hit by human use of the land. Drainage, aimed at providing additional land for agriculture, has removed great areas of marshland formerly available to waterfowl and other wetland animals. Damming of streams, or their canalization, so that the water may be used for agriculture, hydropower, or urban water supplies has removed the habitat for those species that require running streams, yet it has provided new space for those that can adapt to reservoir life. Siltation resulting from overgrazing, deforestation, agricultural or urban use of watersheds has filled in lakes, ponds, and marshes. Aquatic species—particularly fish and amphibians—are more likely to be susceptible to pesticides and other pollutants, and fish-eating birds often accumulate dangerous quantities of these poisons. Filling in of coastal marshes has greatly reduced the space available for estuarine species of animals; coastal pollution, from oil spills or the runoff from land areas can destroy coastal forms of wildlife.

QUANTITY VERSUS INTERSPERSION

It has already been noted that it is often not the quantity of any habitat component that limits the numbers or distribution of animals, but rather its degree of interspersion, or spatial relationship to other requirements. Within any geographic area large quantities of potential food, water, or cover may be unused by some species, simply because they are spaced too far apart in relation to the customary travels of the animal species involved. An animal could potentially travel a very long distance to find water, but it would do little good if it starved or was eaten by a predator during the process.

The complexity of habitat requirements leads to the recognition of the "edge effect" in wildlife management. This means that wherever two habitat types come together, the edge between the two will be more favorable as wildlife habitat than either type considered alone. Both the number of species of animals and the total biomass tends to be larger in the edge area than in any comparable area contained wholly within one or the other type. Aldo Leopold (1933) has stated this as the "law of interspersion." According to this concept, the density of wildlife is directly proportional to the amount of edge, for all species of low mobility that require more than one vegetation type.

The reality of the edge effect becomes apparent to anyone who spends much time in wild country. Extensive uniform forests seem almost lifeless. After traveling through such an area, if one comes out into a streamside woodland or thicket, he or she will be amazed at the variety and abundance of life. Most of the forest dwellers will still be seen, those restricted to stream-side vegetation will be found, the stream dwellers will be there, and in addition those that require a combination of forest, riparian vegetation, and running water will also be present.

LIMITING FACTORS

Many years ago Justus Liebig, a chemist studying plant nutrition, devised the concept of the "law of the minimum." In this he stated that the growth of a plant is dependent on the amount of foodstuff which is presented to it in minimum quantity relative to the needs of the plant. To extend this beyond nutrients—in proportion to the needs of an organism—the requirement that is present in minimum amounts is a limiting factor. Thus, if all other requirements are present in adequate amounts but water is scarce, water will be the limiting factor for wildlife. In such a situation it would be little use to increase amounts of food or cover. Water must be supplied. Liebig's concept applied to those chemical foodstuffs needed for plant growth. Other workers, such as Victor Shelford, have pointed out that too much as well as too little of a particular requirement may also limit the abundance or distribution of a species. There can be too much water in an area as well as too little. Eugene Odum has combined the ideas of previous writers in a statement that any organism requires a complex of environmental conditions and has a range of tolerance to any one of them. Any condition that nears or surpasses the limits of tolerance for that organism becomes a limiting factor for it (Odum, 1972).

Often it is difficult to identify a single limiting factor because an entire complex of conditions is involved. Thus, in one area a lack of escape cover may prevent populations from maintaining themselves above a certain level. Cover could be said to be limiting. However, if predators or hunting were removed, cover would no longer be limiting. If more food or water were available within easy reach of existing cover, higher populations could also be supported. Any one of these factors could be called limiting, and if one were improved, populations might increase. However, further analysis of the situation might reveal that soil nutrients were limiting the growth of food or cover plants, and this lack could not be solved by planting alone. The search for limiting factors can thus become similar to the chase by a dog of its tail.

Although there is little doubt that search for and removal of limiting factors has served to increase wildlife populations, a wildlife manager should remind himself or herself periodically that a total ecosystem is always involved. By concentrating on a single species, and its limiting factor, one can lose sight of the interactions with all other species and the entire system. For example, species A is common but not abundant, and is limited by factor A. Increasing factor A increases species A. But species A is preyed on by species B, which also eats species C and D, which are less abundant than A was originally. When there are more As around, species B increases in abundance to take advantage of its more available prey. Just incidentally it begins to eat more individuals of species C and D, which are then reduced to a critically low level. One could go on tracing more possible interactions resulting from an increase in factor A, but I hope this is sufficient to indicate that oversimplified, single-species approaches to wildlife will not necessarily produce desirable results.

5

INTRODUCING WILDLIFE POPULATIONS

Wildlife populations would be more fun and easier to study if you could only see them. Usually the most you see are individual animals, family groups, and perhaps some flocks, coveys, or herds. Sometimes with gregarious animals it is possible to observe, at least for a time, the entire population. When fur seal herds heave themselves out of the Bering Sea onto the rocky shores of the Pribilof Islands, when sea birds gather on offshore islets, or caribou move through an Arctic pass, the entire local population may be visible. But then they disperse again. With most wildlife, the total population remains an abstraction, something with which biologists and statisticians must grapple. There are, for example, probably no more than 30 condors alive in California at the time I am writing. No person has seen 30 condors, and even the entire team engaged in a condor count does not see the whole population. Nevertheless the size and composition of that population are vital information, since they reveal not only that the species is seriously endangered, but that it continues to decline despite serious efforts to protect and increase its numbers.

A population is defined as the number of animals of a particular species inhabiting a common geographic area. However, as Caughley (1977) has pointed out, there are problems with this simple definition. Much depends on where the area boundaries are drawn and their relationship to the distribution of animals within the general region. The ideal population for study would inhabit an island, or an island-like area, where all individuals would be confined and there would be no problem of movement to or from adjoining populations. In most population studies, however, it is not easy to draw such clear boundaries, but boundary lines should be decided on with relationship to barriers to movement, marked differences in vegetation or terrain, or other characteristics of the environment likely to affect the behavior, movements, or general welfare of the animals involved. Frequently it is not possible to draw meaningful population boundaries until the animals involved have been studied over a period of time and their movements and behavior are well known.

Wildlife biologists and others concerned with the conservation of wildlife must pay attention to individual animals and social groups of animals. The primary area of concern, however, is the population and its characteristics since these can give information concerning the well-being of a particular species that cannot be determined from individual observations. The population has features over and above those of the individual, characteristics that can be measured and described. These include a density, which may change with time; a sex-and-age structure, also altering with time; social organization, natality and mortality rates, and so on. It grows, remains stable, or decreases. It is seldom possible to measure all its characteristics, but for particular purposes some knowledge is essential. If, for example, one wishes to obtain a sustainable yield from a wild animal population, for food, furs, or sport, it is advisable to have knowledge concerning the numbers available and later to be able to measure the effects of the removal of those individuals killed or captured.

To quote Caughley:

> To understand the dynamics of a population we need to know how many animals it contains, how fast it is increasing or decreasing, its rate of production of newborn and its rate of loss through mortality. Properties such as these are called parameters; estimates of parameters are called statistics. A population can be described by an infinite number of parameters but for most purposes a small number is sufficient. The difficulty lies in deciding which to use. (Caughley, 1977)

We will now examine some of these parameters.

DENSITY AND BIOMASS

In an ideal world the starting point for an ecological study of a population would be to determine how many animals were present in the area being studied, and thus to determine their density, expressed as individuals per unit of area. In the real world this starting point sometimes becomes the end point of a population study, and in many studies it is a point not reached at all. Wild animals are not easy to count, not even when they seem to be. Furthermore, it is rarely easy to determine the size of the area occupied. To complicate matters, density is constantly changing as animals are born, die, move into or out of an area. Density must always be referred to a particular time, and density comparisons are useful only as they are related to time. A population may be twice as numerous in early summer, after the young are born, than it will be in early spring when production of young has not yet started. The density of animals in a winter concentration area may be much higher than the density in summer when the animals occupy a much wider range, even if the number of individuals does not change. To be most useful, density should be related to occupied habitat rather than mere geographic area. To be more useful, it should be related to quantity and quality of food, to energy flow through the ecosystem, to the abundance of other species, and other factors equally difficult to measure.

The wildlife literature is filled with papers on census methods, techniques for studying movement and determining size of areas occupied, and related matters. Yet the student who first starts a population study will often feel that all available techniques are inadequate when confronted with apparently invisible animals occupying an opaque habitat. One needs always to ask how easy it is to obtain accurate counts and, having answered that, how necessary is it to have accurate counts. Sometimes indices to relative abundance can be as useful as actual numbers. But since knowledge of actual numbers serves as a check on measurements of all other population parameters, this knowledge should be obtained whenever feasible. Single density measurements or population counts are useful only for comparative purposes. It is the change of numbers over time that is more significant for conversation purposes.

To compare populations of different species, density measurements have limited value. It does not help much to know that an area of African savanna supports one elephant to the square mile, and an area of American grassland, ten pronghorn. For this kind of comparison, *biomass* is usually substituted for density. To determine this, one must calculate the weight of animal life supported, which is the density multiplied by the average weight of the animals being studied—or preferably, but more rarely obtainable, the sum of actual measured weights. Knowledge of biomass permits comparison of species from mice to moose and permits one to draw conclusions concerning relative carrying capacities of widely dissimilar areas. A diagram showing biomass on areas of grassland, desert, and forest is presented in Figure 5.1.

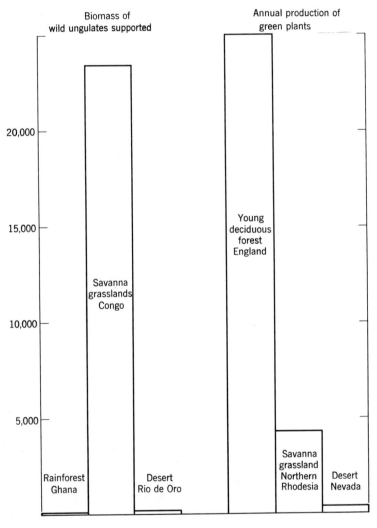

Figure 5.1. Comparison of biomass and productivity for forest, grassland, and desert.

The biomass of animals supported at a particular time is sometimes known as the *standing crop,* a term used most frequently in fisheries biology. This is to be distinguished from *productivity,* which is the rate at which a given population produces new biomass through weight gain or reproduction over a period of time. In Table 5.1 some comparisons of standing crop biomass are

Table 5.1 Population Density and Biomass for Various Species or Species Groups

Habitat and Region	Species	Density (Km^2)	Biomass (kg/km^2)	Reference
Tundra, Canada Average for suitable habitat	Caribou	0.8	ca 60	Banfield (1954)
Tundra, Pribilof Islands. Peak population	Reindeer	18.8	ca 1540	Scheffer (1951)
Tundra, Alaska Cyclic peak	Lemming	12,300	ca 1230	Pitelka (1959)
Chaparral, California. Old growth	Mule deer	11.5	ca 385	Taber & Dasmann (1958)
Tropical dry forest, Zimbabwe	16 ungulate spp.	29.2	3320	Dasmann & Mossman (1962)
Tropical savanna, Zaire	11 ungulate spp.	35.0	29,000	Bourliere & Verschuren (1960)

Table 5.1 (continued)

Habitat and Region	Species	Density (Km²)	Biomass (kg/km²)	Reference
Tropical forest Sri Lanka dry season	Elephant	0.4	650	Eisenberg (1979)
Tropical forest Sri Lanka	Buffalo	1.2	326	Eisenberg (1979)
Marsh, Iowa Cyclic peak	Muskrat	2954	ca 5,000	Errington (1954)
Rainforest Brazil	All animals	—	31,000	Fittkau & Klinge (1973)
Thornbush, East Africa	All animals	—	30,400	Fittkau & Klinge (1973)

presented. In general, the biomass that can be supported depends on the productivity and nutritional value of the vegetation, and this changes with climate and soils. The biomass of animal life also depends on the degree to which the various niches present in an environment are occupied by animal species. The high biomass in the African savanna, for example, does not just represent high productivity of vegetation but also greater use of the available ecologic niches.

In Table 5.1 it may be noted that the larger and more conspicuous animals do not necessarily represent the larger standing crop. Small animals such as lemmings or muskrats may have remarkably high biomasses per unit of area. The very small or microscopic animals found within the soil may also turn out to have a higher biomass than the large and visible animals occupying the ground above. In the Amazonian rain forest, for example, Fittkau and Klinge (1973) determined that there were 165 kilograms per hectare of soil animals, compared to 145 kilograms of all above-ground animal life. In an African thornbush area studied by Hendrichs, the ratio was even more distorted, with 250 kg per hectare of soil animals compared to only 54 kg above the ground (Fittkau and Klinge, 1973).

POPULATION STRUCTURE

At any particular time a wildlife population has a structure determined by the numerical relationships among the ages and sexes of the individuals within it. Some species populations tend to have an even balance between males and females, whereas others, usually because of relatively lower rates of survival of one sex, will have a distorted sex ratio—often more females than males. Some will show a very high percentage of younger age classes, suggesting high productivity but not great longevity. Others will exhibit a more even distribution of age classes. If complete information can be assembled on any population, we can diagram this in the form of a sex and age pyramid, as shown in Figure 5.2. Such a pyramid enables us to analyze the history of a population and to determine its probable future development. A rapidly expanding population will have a pyramid broad at the base because of the high number of young being produced. A population with a stable, slower rate of growth will have a narrower base and taper less sharply toward the top. A declining population will show a narrow base, reflecting a small production of young and a preponderance of older individuals. Irregularities in the shape of a pyramid often indicate the occurrence in the past of unusually favorable or unfavorable conditions for breeding and survival.

If it is difficult to census wild animals, it is far more difficult to determine their population structure. Some animals advertise their sex with bright colors, antlers, or conspicuous sex organs. Others have their sex so thoroughly concealed that humans must dissect their dead bodies or otherwise explore their internal anatomy in order to determine it—although other members of the same species have no difficulty at all in telling the males from the females. Determining age is even more difficult. Usually the very young can be separated out without difficulty, but beyond that age many problems arrive. Techniques have been worked out using rates of change in various anatomical structures: teeth, horns, antlers, eye lenses, ear bones, scales, and so on. Certainty may often require tagging or otherwise marking the young of the year and

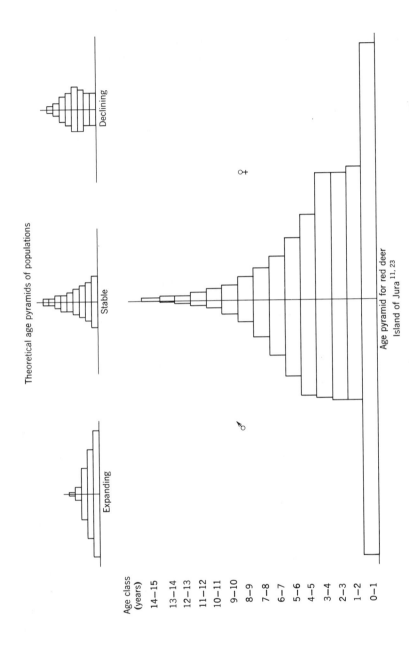

Theoretical age pyramids of populations

Expanding   Stable   Declining

Age class
(years)
14–15
13–14
12–13
11–12
10–11
9–10
8–9
7–8
6–7
5–6
4–5
3–4
2–3
1–2
0–1

♂   ♀

Age pyramid for red deer
Island of Jura [11, 23]

Figure 5.2. Sex-and-age pyramids (Taber and Dasmann, 1957).

following their rates of change and survival over a period of several years. As Caughley (1976) has pointed out, much of the published information must be viewed with some suspicion. That applies to the age pyramid for red deer in Figure 5.2, since there is no way of determining at this time how accurate Evans was in his criteria for age determination.

NATALITY

Changes in a population are brought about by births, deaths, and movement. When these are in balance, the population remains stable in size; when they are out of balance, it grows or declines. The production of new individuals by a population is termed the natality, usually expressed as the number of new individuals born, hatched, or otherwise produced per unit of time (natality rate) or individuals produced per unit of time per breeding individual in the population (specific natality rate). Thus, a quail population could have a total natality of 640 young. Since quail breed seasonally, the unit of time considered is normally 1 year, and the natality rate for the population would be 640 young per year. If these were produced by 80 breeding females, the specific natality rate would be 8 young per year per breeding hen. With big game it is common to express natality rates as numbers of young produced per 100 breeding females per year, as, for example, 80 fawns per 100 does. Natality, in itself, tells much about a population and its relationship to its habitat, and knowledge of it is essential if a population is to be managed actively. Like most population characteristics, however, it is not easily measured. It is influenced by many other characteristics of the species and the population that include the following:

1. Size of clutch or litter produced.

2. Length of breeding season and number of clutches or litters produced per year.

3. Minimum and maximum breeding age for individuals.

4. Sex ratio and mating habits.

5. Population density.

Clutch Size and Litter Size

Species differ greatly in the numbers of young produced by a breeding female in a single laying or birthing period. A condor will have only one egg to a clutch; a turkey vulture, usually two; a quail perhaps 15. Some species, such as the ring-necked pheasant, lay more eggs than they will attempt to incubate. Most African ungulates produce only one young to a litter, whereas many Eurasian and American ungulates produce twins under favorable conditions, and the Chinese water deer is said to produce four fawns as a litter. Clutch or litter size is to some extent determined genetically, so that within a particular species it will not vary greatly from an average number. Thus, a human female usually has one child at a time, and this is considered normal, but twins, triplets, and on up to octuplets have been born. Clutch or litter size is also influenced greatly by the environment. David Lack (1954) noted that robins in Mediterranean Europe have clutches averaging four or five eggs, whereas those in Scandinavia lay six or seven. He related this to the relative availability of food in the two areas. Living in a region with a longer day length during the breeding season, Scandinavian robins have more time for foraging and obtaining food for their young. In most species it has been found that well-situated populations with abundant and nutritious food will have larger litters or clutches than those that suffer from dietary or nutritional deficiencies. Some species will cease to produce young when environmental conditions are unfavorable.

The size of the litter or clutch and the number of young produced during a year varies with the extent to which the species depends on parental care and teaching of the young. Fish may lay thousands of eggs, but each young fish must depend largely on the packet of instincts with which it is born. Parental care can hardly be lavished on hundreds of offspring. A species that takes a long time to mature, and requires a prolonged period of care and training in order to survive, will usually produce a single young, and often will not breed in successive years.

Determination of clutch size or litter size can sometimes be done directly by counting nests and eggs, or locating newly born young animals. Sometimes it must be determined by collecting females and examining the number of embryos or fetuses carried. It can be carried farther back into the breeding cycle by examining ovaries and counting the active corpora lutea, or the scars of corpora lutea from the previous breeding season.

Length of Breeding Season and Numbers of Clutches or Litters per Year

The number of young produced by a population is influenced not only by the size of a clutch or litter, but by the number of times a female will go through a complete breeding cycle during a single year. This in turn is influenced by the length of the breeding season, the gestation or brooding period, the nature of the sexual cycle in the species concerned, and the fate of the preceding clutch or litter.

A species with a short gestation period, such as the meadow vole with a gestation period of 21 days, which also has the capacity to breed immediately after giving birth, could produce spectacular numbers of young. In an average temperate zone breeding season, there would be time for a meadow vole to produce up to 10 litters averaging 6 young per litter, for a total of 60 young. Such high natality would be unusual, of course, since the female must maintain its health and strength throughout the process. At the other extreme, the African elephant has a gestation period of almost 2 years. If they bred immediately after giving birth, they could at best produce 1 calf in 2 years. However, the females apparently do not breed during the period when the young are nursing heavily, and Shortridge (1934) found that they produced at most 1 young in 2½ years, and often at still longer intervals.

Some birds will not usually breed twice in a given year if the first clutch is successfully hatched. If, however, the first clutch is destroyed early in the breeding season, renesting is common among many kinds of birds; but if a clutch is destroyed late in the season, renesting will usually not be attempted. Other species, under favorable conditions, will rear a first brood of young and then go into a second breeding cycyle and produce a second brood.

In the temperate zone most young are produced in the spring, but this is not universal. The grizzly or brown bear will give birth in its winter den at a time when it is not actively feeding (Curry-Lindahl, 1970). Polar bears use winter maternity dens from which they may emerge in late February to move toward the ocean to feed (Jonkel, *et al*, 1970). In the tropics, where there is less seasonal variation than in the temperate zone, some species may breed throughout the year. However, in a single area, some species may display a sharp, distinct breeding season whereas others will not. Thus, in the dry tropics of Rhodesia, zebra and buffalo produce young at any season of the year, but impala and kudu occupying the same locale have sharply defined breeding seasons.

Breeding Age

The number of young produced by a particular population will be influenced not only by clutch or litter size and the numbers of these produced each year, but also by the minimum and maximum breeding ages of individuals in the population. The elephant, for example, does not breed until it is 13 to 14 years of age. Consequently, a high percentage of an elephant herd will be made up of immature, nonbreeding individuals. There is also some evidence that elephants, like humans, survive past their maximum breeding age, so that some part of the population will consist of nonbreeding elders. The total production of young per 100 individuals in the population will therefore appear to be low, since most of the population may consist of nonbreeders. In the same area, the common duiker, a small antelope, breeds and produces its first young by 1 year of age. It is unlikely that many individuals survive past the age of sexual activity. Hence, a duiker population will consist only of breeding adults and young of the year and its percentage of production of young will be relatively high, even though each female will give birth to only a single lamb.

The apparent natality in one population can appear to be higher than in another of the same species only because the former has a lower percentage of nonbreeding young. For example, one deer population could have suffered a catastrophic loss of young in 1980. In 1981, because few yearlings survived from the 1980 crop, almost all females in the population would be breeding age adults. If these produced a good fawn crop in 1981 there might be

150 fawns per 100 does in this population. By contrast, another population could have had excellent fawn survival in 1980 and brought most fawns successfully to yearling age. Since these yearlings would not breed in 1981, the production of fawns per 100 does in the population would appear to be less, even if the adult does in both populations were equally productive. To get at the truth it would be necessary to distinguish adult from yearling females in the field. This is not always possible.

Sex Ratio and Mating Habits

Some wild species are monogamous, some polygamous, some promiscuous; the human species appears to be undecided. The potential natality in a population will be influenced by its breeding habits and by the ratio between the sexes. If a species is monogamous, an equal sex ratio would tend to favor the maximum production of young. For example, quail tend toward monogamous behavior, and a population of 100 quail made up of 25 males and 75 females would have only 25 females laying in a given year. Another population with a 50:50 sex ratio would have 50 laying females, and a higher production of young. A polygamous species, by contrast, would be favored in its production of young by the 25:75 ratio, since 75 females would potentially give birth in a given year, as compared to 50 if the sex ratio were even.

Density

In a sparse population of any species, individuals may have difficulty finding mates and natality may thus be kept at a low level. Once somewhat higher densities are obtained and males and females can locate one another without difficulty, there is often an inverse relationship between natality and density. With increasing density, pressures on the food supply can develop, and the health of breeding individuals may decline. This can result in reduced natality. Even when food or other necessities do not become limiting, social friction can develop at higher densities, which will inhibit breeding—a situation that John Calhoun (1952) discovered in densely crowded colonies of brown rats. Various relationships between natality and density will be examined later, and it will be noted that with some species an inverse relationship does not appear until some threshold density is reached, after which food or other factors interfere with breeding.

Maximum Natality

If all the factors that have been discussed operate in a favorable direction, the natality of a population can reach a maximum. Each species can be said to have a maximum natality rate that can be expressed only under conditions that approach an optimum. This rate allows for the highest sustained production of young.

Great differences in maximum natality rates occur between species. A breeding population of 2 bonito, an ocean fish of the mackerel family, could produce 500,000 young in one season, if all eggs hatched. In the same period two whales, at best, could produce one calf. Bonitos can bounce back from heavy overfishing; whales cannot (Fitch, 1974).

Beluga whales. The slow reproductive rate of these and other cetaceans prevents rapid recovery from overexploitation.

MORTALITY

Just as a healthy wildlife population will reproduce, no population is immune from mortality for long. The causes of death are many, but if all else fails, eventually sheer physiological breakdown through old age will cause the death of the individual. Just as populations have a maximum natality rate, so they could under unusually favorable conditions have a minimum mortality rate, at which old age is the only important cause of death. Usually, however, many other factors come into play first, and it is unusual for a wild animal to die of old age. The factors that cause death have been termed *decimating factors* by Leopold (1933). These are examined in the following sections.

Predation

With most wildlife, predation is an important decimating factor. Predators play a normal role in most, if not all ecosystems. Only isolated populations in areas that predators have not reached—such as some oceanic islands—have escaped predation, along with those populations of the largest herbivores, too big and well defended for predatory attention. For smaller animals predation is an important factor, and with the decreasing size of herbivores the number of predators capable of preying on them will increase. An elk or moose may need only to fear the wolf, but a snowshoe hare needs to watch for owls, hawks, weasel, lynxes, and many others. For the snowshoe hare, therefore, predation is more likely to be a constant and important decimating factor than it is for the larger ungulates.

Predator-prey relationships are affected not only by the relative sizes of the animals involved, but also by the feeding habits of the predators. A generalized predator that feeds on many kinds of prey (the horned owl, for example) can maintain itself even under conditions in which some of its potential prey species are greatly reduced in numbers. On the other hand, a specialized predator that feeds only on one kind of prey is closely tied in abundance to the general level of the population of prey species. Deer populations in the United States support mountain lions, which may feed almost exclusively on deer in some areas. If deer decrease in numbers, mountain lions will usually also decrease.

In predator-prey relationships involving generalized predators, buffering becomes important. A buffer species is essentially an alternate species that serves to decrease predation pressure on another species. For example, an abundant population of wood rats could serve as prey for bobcats that could otherwise feed on cottontail rabbits or quail. In general, the more complex the community, the greater the number of buffer species. In such communities, predator populations can be sustained at a moderately high level by shifting from one type of prey to another, depending on the relative abundance and the ease of capturing each species. When predators are thus maintained at a moderately high level, they can in turn prevent any one kind of prey species from becoming excessively numerous, through feeding more heavily on them.

Although we can speak of generalized and specialized predators, most predators are specialized to some degree, usually feeding only on a certain size range and class of prey. The African lion feeds largely on zebra, wildebeest, and the larger antelope, and does not waste time on the duikers and steenbuck on which the leopard will feed. The balance between energy output and amount of food obtained is highly important to predators. When prey animals are scarce, the energy expended in trying to catch the last few individuals is often more than the food energy to be gained will balance. It is not uncommon for predators to starve when prey becomes difficult to capture.

Diseases and Parasites

In the dry, interior Coast Ranges of California one of the most important diseases affecting deer is called hoof rot. This is caused by an anaerobic bacterium that occurs in the soil, particularly in the mud around watering places for deer. In most years, however, few deer contract this disease. Periodically, in this region, deer numbers, uncontrolled by predation or hunting, build up to a high density. If under these conditions a dry year occurs, and the deer must concentrate around a few water holes, massive die-offs take place. After such a die-off the deer populations are reduced to a relatively low level, the range has an opportunity to make some recovery, and the surviving deer can obtain an adequate supply of nutritious food. They again become relatively free of hoof rot until such time as the range becomes overcrowded once more and dry years force concentration in limited areas (Longhurst, *et al.*, 1952).

Most wild animals at most times are subject to various kinds of infectious diseases and serve as hosts for numerous parasites. Most commonly an adjustment occurs between the host and the disease organism or parasite. When that balance is disturbed, the death of the host can occur. When an entire population is so affected, a major epidemic or epizootic will occur. In natural communities there will normally be many kinds of bacteria, protozoans, viruses, and parasites of other orders to which the bird and mammal species have achieved a mutual adaptation. Should an individual become weakened or injured, and its bodily resistance lowered, disease or parasitism can cause its death. With normal vigor, however, it resists infection. When a population presses on the limits of its food supply and individuals become weakened by malnutrition, diseases or parasites will take their toll. The presence of these organisms can thus serve as a check to prevent excessive habitat destruction by a herbivorous animal, just as predators can prevent a prey population from increasing to the point of habitat destruction.

When a new disease is introduced into a population, however, a different situation prevails. The introduction of myxomatosis, a virus disease of American cottontail rabbits (*Sylvilagus*), into the European rabbit (*Oryctolagus*) populations of Australia and Europe caused the death of millions and almost brought about extermination. The European rabbit lacked the natural immunity the cottontails possessed (Ratcliffe, 1959). However, like most such epizootics, some rabbits escaped because they were more resistant than others. In time their numbers increased, only to encounter newly developed varieties of the disease. One expects an eventual balance similar to the one that prevails with endemic diseases.

In the late nineteenth century an epizootic of rinderpest, a virus disease fatal to various ungulates, spread rapidly over much of the Old World. In Africa the first outbreak was noted in Somaliland in 1889. From there it spread south through the savannas of East Africa and reached Kruger National Park (then the Sabi Game Reserve) in the Transvaal, in 1896. Three years later the epidemic came to an end, and there has been no similar outbreak since. In addition to cattle, many species of wild ungulates were almost eliminated by the disease. In the Kruger area, buffalo were hardest hit, followed by eland, kudu, bushbuck, warthogs, and bush pigs. The sable and roan antelopes and the impala were not affected. Eland, however, were wiped out in the Sabi reserve, and buffalo reduced from thousands to one herd of twenty animals. Immediately following the epizootic the tsetse fly and with it the trypanosomiasis disease of cattle (*ngana*), which is spread from wild ungulates, disappeared from much of the country in Africa south of the Zambesi River. The reasons for this are not known, since many potential host species for the disease survived the epidemic (Stevenson-Hamilton, 1912).

Today, in East Africa, rinderpest still occurs among the wild game, but it now has a role comparable to that of some endemic diseases. Among the wildebeest herds studied by the Talbots (1963), adults are immune to the disease, and the newly born calves have an immunity acquired from their parents. At approximately one year of age, however, this acquired immunity wears off, and heavy mortality among yearling wildebeest takes place from rinderpest. The survivors, however, are immune.

Even among endemic diseases, not all are density dependent in their action. For instance, a major cause of mortality among waterfowl is botulism, brought about by the action of an anaerobic bacterium, *Clostridium botulinum.* In shallow ponds, brackish marshes, or other conditions where decaying vegetation accumulates and oxygen supplies become depleted, the bacteria can thrive. They produce a toxin that enters the water and contaminates food supplies. Waterfowl that ingest the water or food become poisoned and die. Since an entire pond or marsh will become affected, it makes no difference whether one or a thousand ducks use it. All are likely to succumb. Strictly speaking, botulism is a poison rather than a disease. However, some kinds of disease behave in a similar way. Avian malaria was found by Richard Warner to be responsible for the elimination of some species of native Hawaiian land birds. Its principal hosts were introduced exotic birds, and it was spread by an abundant exotic mosquito population. The sparsity of the native bird populations was no defense against the spread of the disease.

Poisoning

I don't know if one can generalize to the extent of saying that wild animals do not usually suffer from naturally occurring poisons. It does seem, however, that over time, species learn to avoid toxic materials that are normally present in their environment.

Many plants produce various toxic alkaloids or other substances that protect them from excessive attacks from herbivorous animals. Animals, in turn, may evolve metabolic mechanisms for neutralizing these toxins, or develop behavioral patterns that cause them to avoid potentially dangerous species. However, the human race has introduced an enormous number of toxic materials into the environment to which wild species have no effective defenses or behavioral adaptations. Use of poisons to control predators, range rodents, and crop-eating birds has long been practiced, with results that have sometimes been severe. The disappearance of the wolf from most of the United States is probably more attributable to the use of poison than to hunting or trapping. More recently, however, the side effects of chemicals introduced into the environment for purposes other than control of wildlife, or accidentally released as pollutants, have had the greatest impact on wild animals. In a review of the effects of toxic substances on wildlife, Risebrough (1978) has identified a number of classes of chemicals that are having, or have had recently, serious effects on wildlife populations. These include sulfur dioxide and nitrogen oxides that contribute to acid rain, which has seriously reduced populations of amphibians and fish in the northeastern United States and Scandinavia, along with many of the plants and smaller animals on which these animals feed. Petroleum in coastal and oceanic waters has had observable and serious effects on marine bird life in particular, along with a variety of other marine organisms. Polychlorinated biphenyls (PCBs), which were originally used widely by industry and are still used in the electric power industry, are apparently having serious effects on wildlife populations, but the evidence to establish these effects, beyond question, is hard to come by. Persistent pesticides, particulary DDE (a derivative of DDT), but also dieldrin, aldrin, heptachlor, chlordane, and other compounds have seriously reduced populations of raptorial birds, and such fish-eating birds as the brown pelican along with a number of other species. Nonpersistent pesticides, such as parathion and the herbicide 2,4,5T with its dioxin contaminant, can also do serious damage. The list of substances is long. Many of them are now banned in the United States, but their use continues, virtually unchecked in some other parts of the world, notably the developing countries of the tropics.

The ultimate effect of these contaminants may be much more

severe for wildlife populations than most of the decimating factors that are discussed. Perhaps it is fortunate that most of those substances toxic to wildlife are also toxic to human beings. Protection of human life and health attracts more public concern than the protection of seemingly obscure forms of wild animal or plant life.

Accidents

Wild animals are no more exempt from accidents than people are. Fires, drowning, falls, highway collisions, and the like can all cause death. At times they can be important to a population. More commonly they are a small, but constant, decimating factor. As populations increase in size and safe shelter is more difficult to find, the likelihood of accidents increases. Where people have introduced many modifications of the habitat—fences, roads, buildings, power line, or other artifacts—they increase the hazards for wildlife. Most frequently, it will be the young, inexperienced members of a population that will fall off a cliff or be hit by a car. Thus, in one deer study it was found that accidents usually happened to fawns, not adults, and most commonly to male fawns. That the same situation occurs in the human species is witnessed by the high rates for automobile insurance charged to young male drivers.

Weather

Weather in the average sense, or climate, limits the ranges of most species. How it operates is sometimes, but not always apparent. A species living in a warm climate may have limited ability for maintaining body temperature. If exposed to cold weather, it will die. One with high water requirements is obviously excluded from deserts except where it can enter along permanent streams. Why a species distribution appears to be halted at a particular climatic line on a map may be difficult to determine. Frequently it is the unusual weather instead of the normal that restricts the distribution of a species.

Weather may have indirect effects on mortality through its influence on food, parasites, predators, or other decimating factors. It may also have direct effects. A sudden hail storm can wipe out a flock of migrating birds. A heavy rain at an unseasonal time can cause mass drowning of young nestlings. An unusual cold spell can reduce temperatures to a point where some species can no longer maintain body temperatures. Thus, weather can have catastrophic effects on populations. The usual effects of weather are not so severe and tend to trim away a population surplus rather than decimate it severely. For example, a pheasant population at a moderate density can find adequate protected nesting sites where the birds may survive the normal weather of the nesting season. An overabundant population, however, will not find enough suitable nest sites. Some birds will nest in more exposed and vulnerable positions where even normal weather can do damage to the eggs or young.

Starvation

When all other decimating factors fail to operate sufficiently to keep a population in check, the habitat exerts a final control. This control is through the food supply, which ultimately will prove inadequate to support the expanding population. Starvation—death resulting from lack of fuel to maintain the metabolic processes of the body—is not common among herbivores, but can occur. It is more common among carnivores. Under such circumstances, animals are forced to draw on their own bodily reserves for energy, and body structures become weakened to the point where normal functioning cannot continue and the animal dies. Most frequently, before actual starvation takes place, the animal will fall victim to some other decimating factor. Starvation remains the important contributing cause of death, although the proximate cause is different.

It was noted earlier that some food factor other than energy may become limiting before a sheer lack of fuel develops. In such circumstances, the animal suffers from malnutrition and its associated weaknesses, which may trigger the action of some other decimating factor. In the absence of these factors, malnutrition leads to starvation and death.

Stress

With some species it has been found that even with an abundance of food, cover, water, and other essentials, excessive numbers alone can be detrimental to a population. Populations increased to high levels have undergone sudden die-offs, during which the endocrine balance of the body is upset and an apparent breakdown of the adrenal-pituitary system occurs. The blood sugar level falls off and the animal dies in a state of shock. Such mortality, called shock disease when discovered in a population of snowshoe hares during a study in Minnesota, has been brought about experimentally in laboratory populations (Green, *et al.,* 1939).

Social stress, brought about by too many contacts and conflicts with other members of a population, causes excessive stimulation of the endocrine system, particularly the adrenal glands. The adrenal cortex will enlarge under these conditions in order to produce sufficient hormones to regulate the body chemistry. A point is reached, however, beyond which further increased production is impossible. When this occurs, an additional social stress, perhaps brought on by weather, the onset of the breeding season, or other factors will cause a sudden, complete breakdown in the endocrine mechanisms and death will result.

The extent to which stress operates in wild populations has been examined in some detail in a paper by Christian (1950), and in captive populations by Calhoun (1952). It has been a subject of some controversy concerning which Brewer (1979) has this summary:

> In some laboratory situations "social pressure" increases as density goes up and has some far-reaching physiological and behavioral effects. . . . A partial list of these includes lowered resistance to disease, failure of females to build proper nests or to nurse young, and even failure of males to produce sperm or females to come into heat. It is certain that these effects befall populations when they get high enough, as in enclosed laboratory situations. What is not clear is how far along this road natural populations go.

Hunting

Predation by man, or hunting, has long been a factor in the dynamics of wild animal populations. Since it is not a simple decimating factor, but a complex of factors, we will examine it more thoroughly in later sections.

Overall Effects of Mortality

In its relationship to a population, mortality is either density dependent, density independent, or some combination of the two.

If it is density dependent, at higher densities a higher percentage of the population will die. Such mortality, through its mode of operation, tends to stabilize a population. A marked increase brings proportionately higher loss; a decrease brings reduced rates of loss. Since most populations of birds and mammals are relatively stable, considering their potential for change, it is believed that mortality among them is more or less density dependent.

Density-independent mortality is not related in its effects to the number of individuals in the population. Hunting, if planned to take a fixed number of animals each year, would be an obvious example of density independence, although most American sport hunting is density dependent in its effects. For natural examples one can look to various catastrophic events—tsunamis, forest fires, ice storms that can devastate a total area and all of its populations, large or small. This type of mortality can have the reverse of a stabilizing effect on populations and cause wide and erratic fluctuations in numbers. Emmel (1973) suggests that density-independent factors are more operative on smaller organisms, such as insects, whereas density-dependent factors are more likely to control bird or mammal populations.

Density-dependent factors are believed to exhibit a compensatory action. That is, if predation should be reduced, other decimating factors such as disease or starvation will increase in their intensity to take its place. With a high level of predation, the amount of loss to disease or starvation is proportionately decreased. Thus, the total action of decimating factors is relatively constant at a particular density level, regardless of the presence or absence of single factors that can cause death. This idea is basic to understanding the role of hunting as a management tool, and will be given more detailed consideration in a later section.

Mortality and survival in a population can be presented in the form of a life table (Table 5.2). A given age class, of 1000 individuals, is followed in this table through its life span until the last individual has died. The mortality rates in each year and the life expectancy of the surviving individuals are shown. The table is based on populations of black-tailed deer studied over many years in which most individuals were well known. It is not particularly easy to obtain such information from most wild populations. If the two authors of this particular study had realized that they had

Table 5.2   Life Table for Black-Tailed Deer of Chaparral (Females) (Taber and Dasmann, 1958)

Age Class in Years (x)	Number Alive at Start of Age Interval (1_x)	Number Dying during Age Interval (d_x)	Rate of Loss (No. Dying per 1000 in Population) (q_x)	Life Expectancy for Age Class (e_x)
0–1	1000	372	372	4.2
1–2	628	41	65	5.3
2–3	587	66	112	4.6
3–4	521	68	131	4.2
4–5	453	67	148	3.7
5–6	386	54	140	3.1
6–7	332	54	163	2.6
7–8	278	54	194	2.0
8–9	224	33	147	1.4
9–10	191	191	1000	0.5

Note: This form of life table follows a given year class of 1000 individuals through until the last individual has died. In the 1_x column the number of individuals of the original 1000 that still survive to the stated age is shown. In the d_x column the number of individuals that were found to die during that particular year of life is given, and in the q_x column this is converted into the rate of loss, number dying per 1000 in the population. In the e_x column the life expectancy of a deer in a given age class is given. Note that a deer that lives through the critical first year of life has a higher life expectancy than a young fawn; note also that very few yearling deer die. The loss in the 9–10 year class is exaggerated. The available techniques did not permit age determination beyond 10 years of age; hence many older deer are lumped into the 9–10 year class.

better things to do with their time, this particular life table would not have been prepared.

INTERACTION OF POPULATION CHARACTERISTICS

When the density of a population is low by comparison with the capacity of the environment to support it, the population will usually increase. Mortality will be relatively light and natality rates will be high because all individuals can find suitable cover, food, and other necessities. Each population has a theoretical maximum growth rate that is referred to as its *biotic potential.* For it to be fully expressed, all the factors favoring natality will be operating in a favorable direction, whereas the decimating factors, because of the abundance of the necessities of life, will be little evident. Such ideal conditions are sometimes, but rarely, realized over short periods.

Usually biotic potential should be calculated by considering the actual performance of populations under field conditions that approach an optimum as closely as we can determine it for that species in question. Conditions that can be experienced by well-fed captive populations may provide useful information about physiological capacities of a species, but may never be encountered in wild populations.

Any species, continuing at a biotic potential rate of increase, could in a remarkably short time crowd the entire world with its progeny. No species does this because no habitat is unlimited. Inevitably, decimating factors will take their toll. The sum total of all decimating factors that cause mortality, combined with those habitat factors that decrease natality, is known as the *environmental resistance*. It is the resistance of the environment to an unlimited increase of a species population. The growth, decline, or stability of a population can be regarded as the resultant of the action of two forces: biotic potential, leading to unlimited, rapid increase, and environmental resistence, causing mortality or reducing natality, and therefore preventing the biotic potential from being realized. When these two forces are in balance, a population is stable. When one is out of balance with the other, a population grows or declines.

Turnover

Many wildlife populations display a remarkable degree of stability. If measured at the same time each year, it will often seem that there are just about the same number of wren-tits, or red-tailed hawks, or towhees as there were the year before. Stable, however, does not mean static. No population is static. Mortality and natality go on, year after year; individuals die and are replaced by new individuals.

Few wild animals live to be old. A deer could live to be more than 20 years of age, and some do. In the wild, most deer at birth have an average life expectancy of 2 or 3 years. Heavy juvenile mortality often takes place, since the young are more vulnerable.

This alone brings the average life span for a population down to a low level. No age class, however, is immune to mortality, and the total mortality in any stable population must balance the total natality. There is consequently a *turnover* in populations—individuals change, although numbers remain the same. The rate of replacement of old individuals by new is the *turnover rate*. It is usually measured by determining the percentage of young in the population, compared to adults, at the start of a breeding season. A quail population, approximately stable at 100 birds, may be found in the fall hunting season to contain seventy young of the year, and thirty older birds. During the year, therefore, there was a turnover of 70 percent of the population, with the death of 70 birds from the preceding year's population.

Turnover rates of 70 percent or higher are not unusual among birds and small mammals. Among larger birds and mammals turnover rates of 20 to 40 percent are common. Species with a high biotic potential, experiencing high environmental resistance, have high turnover rates. A musk-ox population, with low biotic potential and few effective enemies will have a much lower turnover rate than a population of arctic hares.

Productivity

A distinction between standing crop and productivity was considered in an earlier section. The potential productivity of a population, or capacity to increase, is determined by its biotic potential. The actual, or realized, productivity depends on realized natality and on growth and survival of young.

The productivity of an animal population is termed secondary productivity, to distinguish it from the productivity of green plants (primary productivity). One depends on the other.

Primary productivity is the rate at which new organic matter is added to an ecosystem, mostly by green plants, from the inorganic materials of the environment.* A young growing forest has a high rate of productivity because of the rapid growth of young trees. A mature forest, in which growth rates have slowed, will

---

*It is useful to distinguish gross primary productivity, which is the total amount of new organic material resulting from photosynthesis, from net primary productivity, which reflects the losses from respiration during that same period. This discussion refers to net productivity.

have a lower rate of productivity. In the young forest, productivity will be greatly in excess of mortality. In the mature forest, mortality may equal or at times exceed productivity.

Secondary productivity is the rate at which new animal biomass is added to an ecosystem. It is usually measured as the rate at which animal populations produce new individuals of breeding age, and thus reflects both natality rates and survival and growth of young animals.

Declining secondary productivity reflects decreased natality; growth or survival of young and often indicate that a population is pressing on its means of subsistence. In theory, such a population can be stimulated to increased productivity by hunting. If excess individuals are removed, the survivors obtain more food and space, and their productivity increases. In practice, this often works but sometimes it does not. We will look into this in a later section.

6

TERRITORY AND TRAVELS

Everybody knows that wild animals move around. Fewer people know that most of them like to stay at home in familiar territory and only move out when forced to go. The travels of wild animals have long held a fascination for those who observe them. The sudden appearance of hosts of waterfowl in an area where previously there had been none, the arrival of masses of moving lemmings in the Arctic, or the passing of the great herds of springbuck in southern Africa have given rise to folklore and mythology. Some wildlife travels are spectacular. Golden plovers leave Alaska and fly nonstop across the Pacific to land on the islands of Hawaii—a tiny land target in a vast oceanic expanse. Humpback whales depart from the Antarctic waters each year and, without the aid of high technology, locate their regular breeding ground in the seas of Tonga. But it is equally curious that other birds with potentially great flying ability stay most of the time in their own "backyards."

What happens to an animal population depends not just on the rate of births or deaths, but also on the extent to which animals move into or out of populations. Only those populations on oceanic islands or those otherwise restricted by impassable barriers are relatively unaffected by movements. All others are influenced to some extent. The frequency with which animals travel and the distances they go vary with the species and the kind of environment in which it occurs. Some kinds of movement, involving individuals instead of flocks or herds, are difficult to detect.

Most studies of wildlife travels depend on the marking of individuals in such a way that they can be recognized wherever they appear.

The travels of animals can be considered under two categories: those internal to the area occupied by the population, which do not affect the composition of the population, and those external to the population area that take individuals out of or bring them into the population and thus change its composition. In the first category are both the relatively short daily travels of an individual within its home area, and the mass movement of an entire population from one portion of its range to another. In the second category are those travels known collectively as *dispersal,* which establish new populations and result in the colonization of new areas.

MOVEMENTS INTERNAL TO THE POPULATION AREA

Home Range

If the travels of an individual are closely observed and the areas visited and distances traveled are charted, it will be found for many species of animals that movements are much more restricted than one would surmise from consideration of the animal's capacity to travel swiftly over long distances. Frequently, much of its activity will center around some favored feeding ground, or a place where it rests or sleeps, or perhaps a patch of cover in which it feels secure from enemies. This area, its *center of activity,* may be quite small (Haynes, 1949). Around it will be a somewhat larger area that it visits occasionally—different feeding grounds, resting places, and escape cover, but even this larger area will be of such a size that it could be crossed by the animal in a short time and with little effort. This area in which an individual animal spends all, or most of, its time is known as its *home range.* Not all species have small home ranges, but a surprising number do. Obviously, there are advantages to spending as little energy as possible in search of food and in knowing just where to hide if a predator appears, or in having a familiar place to avoid extremes of weather or insect attacks. The animal in a strange place is at a disadvantage, and less likely to survive.

This author and others have studied home ranges in the mule

deer species. Although these animals could travel dozens of miles across country in a day, with little strain, it was found in most instances that their entire year-round travels were restricted to an area less than a square mile in size, and that most of their activity was within a smaller area, perhaps a quarter-mile in diameter (Fig. 6.1). These home ranges contain all the food, shelter, escape cover, and other needs for the individuals that occupy them. Within a home range a deer knows the travel routes and can quickly reach any kind of cover it requires. Efforts to drive deer from their home ranges have been generally unsuccessful. Deer transplanted to other areas tend to head back for home. In some cases deer have died from malnutrition within a home range when by moving a half-mile or more outside of it they could have found adequate food. The attachment to a home area is strong, and its boundaries appear well known to the animal.

Migratory deer have two different home ranges, one for winter and one for summer. Between these they travel over a clearly defined migration trail. Some prefer to regard this as a single, elongated home range that thins out in the middle to the width of the migration route. The size of a home range varies with the

Figure 6.1. Home range of a tagged black-tailed doe, 1951-1955. Dots indicate individual sight records.

spacing of food, cover, water, and other essentials, but if these are too widely spaced the area will not be occupied.

Migration

Migration is a two-way movement within the area normally occupied by a species population. The word should not be (but frequently is) confused with immigration or emigration, which are forms of dispersal. Migration commonly represents travel from one seasonably suitable habitat to another, with a subsequent return to the first. In migration an entire bird population will leave its breeding ground and fly perhaps thousands of miles to a wintering ground—the same breeding ground, and the same wintering ground each year. The navigational problems involved in such migrations have long been a subject for research.

Banding studies carried out over many years by the United

More precise knowledge of flyways has facilitated the restoration of the formerly endangered trumpeter swans.

States Fish and Wildlife Service, state game departments, and co-operating bird banders have revealed that most birds follow regular migration routes, or *flyways,* each year. In some ingenious studies carried out by Bellrose, Hamilton, and others, it has been shown that migrating birds are able to orient and steer by sun and star positions, although they may use local landmarks to aid in reaching a particular spot after they have attained the general geographic locality by celestial navigation. Birds confined in a planetarium during the season of migration attempt to move in the directions indicated by the artificial star patterns presented by the planetarium sky.

Flyways are now sufficiently well known to serve as a basis for waterfowl management, although the situation is more complicated than people believed in earlier decades (Fig. 6.2). Hunting regulations are tailored to the size and productivity of the populations using a particular flyway. A reduction in one flyway through overshooting or some other cause need not necessarily affect the regulations for another flyway for which no such problem has developed.

Mammal migrations and the travels of marine reptiles such as sea turtles can be equally as spectacular as those of birds. The travels of fish have long attracted interest, particularly those that return somehow to the same home stream after roaming thousands of miles in the open ocean. On land, the caribou of the American arctic and the wild reindeer of the Soviet tundra today follow long migratory pathways that take them as far as 800 miles between summer and wintering grounds. Both caribou and, formerly, the American bison exhibit a degree of *nomadism,* or irregular long-distance movement. Portions of a range may be abandoned and not revisited for many years. The entire population will shift to a new region, there to take up once more a new migration pattern. Some African mammals also exhibit irregular travel patterns. The Talbots (1963) have described the movements of wildebeest in the Serengeti-Mara area of East Africa. These appear to be influenced by local rainfall, fires, and the consequent availability of new grass, and may differ greatly from year to year.

Wherever there are high mountains, many of the animals living on them will exhibit an up-and-down mountain migration between summer and winter range. In some instances this will in-

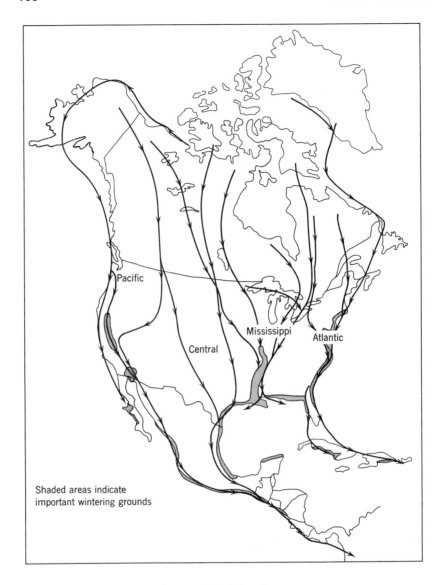

Figure 6.2. Major water fowl flyways of North America.

volve a shift of only a few miles, but in other populations such as the migratory deer of northeastern California and southern Oregon, a hundred miles may separate the extremes of summer and winter ranges (Salwasser, 1979).

The benefits of migration to animals are apparent. Migration permits a population to take advantage of food and shelter provided by an area that is only seasonally habitable. Few birds can withstand the rigors of an Arctic winter, but millions find breeding grounds and feeding areas there during the productive summer months. The same millions can find winter food and shelter in the southern United States and tropical America, but might have difficulty in finding suitable breeding areas in this region. How did the present patterns of migration evolve? It is easy enough to figure out why deer move up and down a mountain, yet not so easy to guess how sea turtles learned to find one particular tiny island on a planet that is mostly covered with ocean.

MOVEMENTS EXTERNAL TO THE POPULATION AREA

If all animals stayed at home or moved only along fixed and predictable migration routes there would not be many animals on earth. In fact animals turn up in strange and unexpected places—from the center of big cities to continents on which they are not "supposed to be." There are few places that flying birds or bats can't reach if the winds are right and they happen to be carried off their normal course. But geckos and skinks (lizards that don't fly and can't swim well) have reached the far Pacific Islands, along with frogs that don't tolerate salt water. Of course, people carry animals to a lot of places, either deliberately or otherwise, but animals have colonized most of the earth's surface without human assistance.

Dispersal movements fall into two categories, depending on how you look at them: immigration, which is movement *into* a new area, and emigration, which is movement *out of* a previously occupied area. A single animal on one journey can be both an emigrant and an immigrant. Either type of movement can be important in determining the balance of a population. A population at a low level can increase more rapidly than would be expected from natality alone through immigration from surrounding areas of high density. With some species, dispersal substitutes for mortality as a mechanism that relieves overcrowding. Most frequently it will be young individuals, not settled in a home range, that will disperse. In some instances, however, other age classes will be involved.

The factors that cause dispersal are not always known. Sometimes an obvious antagonism develops between parents and young as the young reach maturity. In other instances, fighting between adult individuals can force one adult to leave the home area. In Errington's studies of muskrats in Iowa marshes (1954), dispersal was found to be one of the most important mechanisms for population regulation. Each spring the young muskrats are driven from the lodges by the adults and, unless they can find unoccupied ground within the home marsh, are forced to travel over unsuitable terrain in search of space in other marshes. Such dispersing individuals readily fall to predation or succumb to accidents along the way.

Sometimes adult individuals with an established home range will leave that home, often for reasons that are not apparent, and drift off to some new area. In some instances, after a sojourn in distant areas, the individual will return to its home ground once more. This kind of *wandering* was observed among adult black-tailed deer in California, and the reasons for it could not be explained. It was unusual and in apparent contradiction to normal behavior—the bear that "went over the mountain to see what he could see" comes to mind.

Dispersal permits a species to spread to new areas, and is essential for the survival of species confronted with severe environmental change. It permits the exploitation of new habitats and thus protects the species when old habitats become unsuitable or are destroyed. Dispersal rates and tendencies vary greatly among species. In New Zealand, for example, the introduced red deer spread quickly throughout the two main islands, occupying most areas of suitable habitat. By contrast, the fallow deer, sika deer, and white-tailed deer, although surviving well in the area into which they were first introduced, have failed to spread at the same rate (Wodzicki, 1961).

Sometimes it is the apparent failure to disperse and colonize that raises questions and can cause conservation problems. Diamond (1979) has noted that in species-rich environments in the humid tropics, bird distribution is patchy. Areas of apparently suitable habitat are unoccupied by a species that may be abundant in areas on either side, even when that species has a broad tolerance for habitat variation. The explanations advanced for this phenomena are not entirely satisfactory. It does mean that reserves intended to protect the entire spectrum of rain-forest avi-fauna may fail to contain certain species that would usually be expected in such habitats.

GROUP SIZE AND SPACING

Within an area occupied by a population, individuals will be disposed in various ways. Some species show a strong tendency toward social aggregation. These species may travel in flocks or herds or form colonial groups that settle in a restricted area. At times an entire population may be found in a single herd, moving together from one portion of a range to another. With many ungulates, however, sex-and-age segregation in groups is common, and the same phenomenon may be seen among marine mammals and waterfowl. Among elk, under the leadership of an old cow, cows and calves will form a herd that will stay together through the years. Young bulls may join a cow herd or move in a separate group. Older bulls often form a smaller band, separate from the cows, and only join them during the rut. In the rutting season a bull will attempt to form a separate "harem" and defend it against all comers. Usually the herd bull will be replaced by a different animal as the rutting season progresses, and that in turn by still another, often to the accompaniment of strenuous battles between the competing bulls.

Some species of rodents (ground squirrels and prairie dogs, for example) live a colonial existence, digging their burrows in a common area. These gain an advantage from the greater ability of the group to modify and maintain the vegetation. The colony can keep a grassland in a successional stage favoring the existence of the group. The individuals in a colony also gain some security from predation through having many lookouts to warn of a hunting coyote or fox (Koford, 1958).

Large social aggregations are most often seen among species that occupy open terrain, whereas smaller social groups are most frequent among dwellers in forest or brush. There are exceptions. Monkeys, coatis, and parrots that dwell in tropical forests often occur in large aggregations. In the marine environment, the larger schools of fish seem characteristic of the open, pelagic environment of the oceans, whereas in the complex environment of a coral reef one may encounter hundreds of species of fish, but relatively few individuals of each species.

Among animals that do not form large social aggregations, some species—the bobcat, for example—will occur singly and usually only come together for mating. A female and her young will be the largest social group. Other species are more gregarious, occurring in family bands that include young of the year and subadults. Among those species that occur singly or in small groups, some such as black-tailed deer show no strong tendency to avoid other individuals or groups. Their movements within an area will mostly be governed by the environment rather than by particular reference to the presence or absence of others. Other species, however, may show a distinct mutual intolerance or antagonism toward one another, and their movements and spacing will be governed in part by mutual avoidance.

TERRITORY

Animals that exhibit antagonism toward other members of their species will often space themselves within a habitat in such a way that contacts between individuals are minimized. When this results in the occupancy of an area by an individual or a group to the usual exclusion of other individuals or groups of the same species, the area occupied is known as a *territory,* and the behavior that leads to such exclusive, or near exclusive, occupancy and spacing of home areas is known as *territorialism.* Like so many other terms in wildlife biology, however, these words are used in different senses. The British have used territory to mean home range, whereas Americans have used it in the sense defined here (Wilson, 1971). Attempts to reconcile these two definitions create greater confusion.

Territoriality was first investigated among birds (Howard, 1920). In some species, the male will stake out a home area at the start of a breeding season and defend it against all other males. If he succeeds in attracting a female to the area, the two will mate and nest. The boundaries of the territory will be proclaimed vigorously by the male's singing from conspicuous perches around its edges. Other males will usually respect these proclamations, but if they don't, fighting will result. Most commonly the intruder will be driven off. Such active aggressive behavior among birds led to the concept of a territory as a defended area (Nice, 1941). Subsequent studies of many other animals have produced the realization that territorialism is widespread and not confined to birds. With some species, active aggression or defense is rare. The individuals or groups maintain their spacing through mutual intolerance without the need for fighting. From an ecological viewpoint, it is the spacing that is important rather than the behavior that accomplishes this end.

Territorialism can serve as a mechanism to prevent the overcrowding of a habitat, and thus guarantee to each individual or territorial group a space within which its necessities are available and are maintained for its exclusive use. Territoriality would thus provide a greater security for the species, and it would be expected that such populations would display greater stability than those of species lacking such a behavioral pattern. In Emmel's words (1973),

> *We can see a nice example of this effect of territorial behavior in Howler Monkey* (Alouatta villosa) *populations inhabiting the lowland forests of the New World tropics. A small population group of these monkeys travels around as a unit, maintaining a "core" of territory against all other Howler groups. It does this by communal howling in the early morning hours, which warns other groups of Howlers of their presence near a defended territory . . .*

Brewer (1979) points out that

> *If there is room for about five pairs of scarlet tanagers in a 20-acre oak forest, there is likely to be about five pairs there, no matter how many are seeking to occupy the space. If numbers are high there will be some chasing, a lot of singing, and perhaps a little actual fighting early in the spring. Within a few days the situation will settle down, with about five pairs occupying territories. What of the other birds, the surplus? Several possible fates await them, most of which will reduce possibilities for survival and production of young as compared with the birds who won out. They may emigrate to less favorable habitat and breed, probably producing relatively few young because the habitat is unfavorable. They may not be able to establish territories at all but may simply form a floating, nonbreeding population.*

However, as Watson and Moss have pointed out (1970), there are conditions that must be established before we can say that territorialism is actually limiting populations. First, we must know that the breeding population of territorial animals is not in fact using up some resource, such as food. If it is, the resource is limiting, not the territorial behavior. There must also be a nonbreeding surplus of population, some of which at least must be capable of occupying a territory and breeding if the dominant territorial animals are removed—that is, if territorial behavior is limiting, it must have the effect of reducing numbers, or reducing the amount of breeding that takes place.

Many different kinds of territories have been reported. Some species, the robin, for example, become territorial only during the breeding season and at other times may flock together. Other species, such as the wren tit, will maintain sizable territory throughout the year and drive off any encroaching strangers. You don't see large flocks of wren tits, or of wrens either. Colonial nesting birds do not maintain feeding territories, but they will defend a space immediately around their nests. Some mammals have herd or pack territories. David Mech (1970) has described pack territories among wolves: "In a sense, aggression between unassociated wolves could also be regarded as defense of a range or territory, or at least it would have the same effect. On this basis, one could conclude that wolf packs are territorial to the extent that their territories include most of their hunting and travelling areas. If this is true, it would be expected that packs would become spaced throughout a range in such a way as to avoid or minimize meeting other packs." He further points out that on Isle Royale in Lake Superior, the principal wolf pack used the entire island to some extent. Other wolves fitted themselves into space used least by the dominant pack. In later studies (Peterson, 1977), when two primary wolf packs occupied Isle Royale, each occupied about half the island with little overlap.

M. G. Hornocker (1969) and later John Seidensticker and his co-workers (1973) have studied social organization, including territoriality among mountain lions. Areas occupied by individual lions are large, but differ from one another with one lion occupying a yearly area of 173 sq km, whereas another occupies 453 sq km in the Idaho Primitive Area. "Resident male home areas overlapped but little. Those of resident females often overlapped completely and were overlapped by resident male areas. Transient lions of both sexes moved about these areas. . . . Land tenure was based on prior right, but the system was not static. Home areas were altered in response to the death or movement of other residents. Young adults established residences only as vacancies became available." Seidensticker, *et al.* prefer not to use the term territory or territoriality; however, the behavior that they describe appears to fit this category. They note that lions do not readily seem to colonize new areas, or reinhabit areas such as Yellowstone National Park, from which they had previously been eliminated. Apparently, the dispersing young lions seek areas in the vicinity of other lions to establish new territories. They may travel through large unoccupied areas, but are unlikely to remain. This would, of course, reduce the ability of this species to recover from the effects of predator control, or heavy hunting.

Some further ideas on territory and density will be discussed in a later chapter.

SIGNIFICANCE OF SPACING AND MOVEMENTS

It is obviously not enough to study natality and mortality in a population to understand its dynamics. In addition, one must take into account the extent to which the population is affected by movements and the innate behavior of the species involved. Many years ago, Leopold noted that despite all habitat improvement, it appeared to be impossible to increase bob-white quail above a density of approximately one bird per acre. Territorial behavior and dispersal operated to hold densities at this level, sometimes referred to as a "saturation point." The wildlife manager may be puzzled by failures of such populations to increase, but without studies of behavior and movements one is unlikely to understand the reasons.

The management of migratory species is usually more difficult than that of resident game. Improvement of habitat on a summer range will not benefit a population for which some element on the winter range is limiting. During the 1930s, drought caused a great reduction of breeding grounds for waterfowl in the northern prairies of the United States and Canada. The numbers of ducks and geese moving down the Mississippi flyway were reduced and hunting regulations had to be changed to provide additional protection. The populations on the Pacific flyway, with breeding grounds in the Alaskan tundra were less affected and did not need the same degree of protection. In 1976–77 the drought in California and the Southwest had the reverse effect, and if it had continued for one more year the populations wintering in that area would have been drastically affected. Lack of adequate wintering space and winter food supplies are much more likely to be a problem for Pacific flyway ducks than for the Mississippi waterfowl.

Restoration of populations of the trumpeter swan and whooping crane has depended on a detailed knowledge of summer breeding grounds, migratory routes, and wintering areas, so that these threatened species could be protected at all stages of their life cycle. But despite all studies, conservationists operate in areas in which some factors are beyond their control. In 1979, the whooping crane, carefully nurtured through captive breeding and strict protection of its wild population, had its wintering ground threatened by the worst oil pollution in recorded history—the outpouring of a Mexican well drilled in the Gulf of Campeche hundreds of miles away.

7

TOO MANY MICE, TOO FEW ELEPHANTS

Some time ago one of the best known cartoonists in the United States was Rube Goldberg. He specialized in designing elaborate devices to do simple jobs. Moving a marble one inch would probably require, at a minimum, a squirrel on a wheel, two candles, a trained mouse, numerous pulleys, and yards of string. At the other extreme was a gentleman named William of Ockham, who in the fourteenth century stated a principle variously known as the law of parsimony, or Ockham's razor (for shaving the fuzziness off thinking). It stated essentially that if several different explanations will fit all of the known facts, the simplest explanation must be accepted. This principle is supposed to guide all scientific investigation, and one must always seek the simple solution that adequately takes care of the facts. Nevertheless, in the dark of night, some wildlife biologists suspect that ecosystems were actually designed by Rube Goldberg. Herbert Baker, who knows a great deal about botany, plant ecology, evolution, and the tropics, warns that nature's methods are not necessarily simple, and that it is possible for several different explanations to be equally true "even for the same groups of organisms in the same places at the same times" (Baker, 1970). All of which is a way of observing that the study of wildlife population dynamics can be sticky and confusing.

There are reasons for studying wildlife populations other than the sheer joy of doing it. One may wish to increase the population of a species threatened with extinction or to decrease the population of one that has made itself a pest. Often one wants to determine how to crop a population, or harvest it, in such a way that it will go on yielding a crop forever—that is, to determine a safe, sustainable yield. One may also not desire to do anything to a population except to see that it is relatively safe and secure, and not likely to destroy its own habitat. To do any of these things, it is necessary to know something about population dynamics. There are many hypotheses and models used to explain changes in wild-life populations. Some of them contradict others. Under some circumstances all of them might be true, or—what is perhaps more important—useful.

NEW POPULATIONS IN NEW HABITATS

Wildlife biologists become involved, not infrequently, with introducing a species into a new area, or reintroducing an old one into a habitat that has been unoccupied for a long time. This practice can be carried out in an attempt to provide more, or a greater variety of, hunting or fishing; or it can be implemented to safeguard or increase a threatened species. Assuming that the habitat is favorable, one will expect the population to increase. So long as numbers are low in relation to the availability of food, cover, and water—and if predators are not too abundant—the new population can be for a time almost free from mortality. With an abundance of food and space, the birth rate can be high, and the rate of increase will approach the biotic potential. With a small initial stock, however, even with a high rate of increase, total numbers will remain low for a while, since doubling a population of 2 only gives 4 and doubling 4 only gives 8. Thus, the initial changes in population may be difficult to detect in the field and there may not be much evidence that the introduction is succeeding. However, as the size of the breeding population and the annual crop of young begins to grow, the total numbers pyramid from year to year (doubling 200 makes 400). If the numbers of animals are plotted on graph paper as a curve, there will be an initial period when the curve is relatively flat (climbing from 2 to 4 to 8 to 16), followed by a period when it bends steeply upward (32 to 64 to 128, etc.). However, as the limits of the environment are approached, it can be expected that mortality will increase. Some animals perhaps will not obtain enough food; others, exposed in their search for food, will more easily be taken by predators; others, weakened by food deficiencies, may become vulnerable to disease-causing bacteria or other pathogens. As the breeding females fall off in condition, through lack of food or disease, a decrease in natality will follow. The closer the population comes to the capacity of the environment, the greater the influence of decimating factors will become. Consequently, the curve of population growth will be bent downward further, and eventually may level off to a point where birth and death rates are in balance. This point will represent the capacity of the habitat to support animals of that species.

If factors really do operate in this way, the curve of population growth will have a characteristic "S" or sigmoid shape that resembles a curve obtained by plotting the logistic equation originally calculated by Pearl and Reed (1920) in an attempt to predict human population growth in the United States. If Pearl and Reed's calculations had come true, we would in 1980 have a U.S. population of 175 million, and this would slowly increase to a stable level of 198 million, more or less. Unfortunately, the U.S. population in 1980 is nearer 230 million and still climbing. However, the logistic equation has its uses and is expressed as follows:

$$\frac{\Delta N}{\Delta t} = rN \left(\frac{K - N}{K} \right)$$

The sight of such an equation causes some people to enter into a state of acute mental paralysis, since it is drawn from the dreaded field of calculus, but it can be easily understood. It says that a growth of population is determined by the biotic potential as modified by the environmental resistance. To go further in this exercise, we will need to use some of the symbols from the equation:

N = total population

t = time

r = maximum potential rate of increase (or increase in numbers of individuals per unit of time per individual in the population)

K = Carrying capacity or total numbers habitat can support

The expression $\Delta N / \Delta t$ is the increase in numbers per unit of time (change in N over change in t). The expression rN, the biotic potential, gives you the numbers of individuals produced in the given time period, without environmental resistance. If a population produces one young per year, for each male and female pair, the value of *r* is .5 and *rN* is .5 × 2 or 1 young per year assuming all animals are reproductively active and the sex ratio is 1:1. $K - N/K$, the environmental resistance, is near unity when the population is low, which means that the biotic potential is expressed with little modification. However, as the numbers (N) increase to the level of K, the value of this expression approaches and eventually equals 0. *rN* multiplied by 0 equals 0, the rate of growth at carrying capacity.

The logistic equation represents a mathematical model of a population. The statement that the growth of a population is determined by its biotic potential proportionally reduced by the environmental resistance is a conceptual model. Models are useful for understanding populations, but they are always oversimplifications of reality. Just as one can use infinite care in building a cardboard model of a house, that model will not be like the house, and its usefulness may be confined to giving you some idea of spatial relationships, but will hardly apply to the house's structural strength. So too are mathematical or conceptual models useful for certain purposes, but one cannot lean too heavily on them. The logistic equation is a simple model of population dynamics under certain circumstances. Although it is a faulty model for bird and mammal populations, for many reasons that will be examined, it still reflects reality to this extent—population growth in many wild species often exhibits an S-shape when plotted on a graph: an initial slow growth (although the rate of increase is high), followed by a period of rapid numerical increase (although the rate of increase may be declining), followed by a rough sort of levelling off with minor fluctuations. If you were to use this formula to predict the growth of a wild turkey population you had just turned loose, you would be extremely fortunate to come as close as Pearl and Reed in their estimate of U.S. population growth.

There are certain built-in assumptions in the logistic formula that need consideration (Brewer, 1979): (1) It assumes complete density-dependence in mortality or, in other words, a straight line relationship between increasing density and its unfavorable effects; (2) it assumes continuous natality and mortality, a situation that applies to yeast cells in a bottle, or *Paramecium* in a laboratory culture, but not to birds and mammals in the wild; (3) it assumes that every individual in a population is the same, which is hardly true for populations with two sexes and delayed maturity. Nevertheless, with some modifications to take these factors into account, I have used the logistic curve to show the growth of a mule deer population (Table 7.1 and Figure 7.1). This is a revealing exercise, since in this modified logistic, certain effects are emphasized. Thus, it is year 4 before the population first departs from the rate of increase predicted from the assumed biotic potential; in other words, there is an initial period when environmental resistance is not felt. Note also that in year 8, the annual increment to the population is at a maximum, or the greatest numerical increase is attained. In this year the population is approximately 50 percent of what it will be at carrying capacity. This particular point, an inflection point in a curve, is the controversial point of

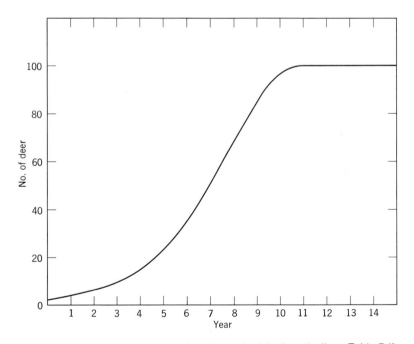

Figure 7.1. Increase in mule deer based on a logistic formula (from Table 7.1).

**Table 7.1 Increase in a Mule Deer Population Based on a
Logistic Formula**

Year	Breeding Population Females N_b	Total Population, N_t	Annual Increment, $\Delta N/\Delta t$
1	1	2	2
2	1	4	2
3	2	6	4
4	3	10	5
5	5	15	9
6	8	24	11
7	12	35	16
8	18	51	17
9	26	68	16
10	34	84	11
11	42	95	4
12	48	99	1
13	50	100	0

Formula: $\Delta N/\Delta t = rN_b \dfrac{K - N_t}{K}$

Assumptions: K, carrying capacity, equals 100 deer. r, maximum rate of increase is two fawns
per breeding female.
Sex ratios are equal.
Does produce first fawns at two years of age, thereafter annually.

Note: In year 4 the population first departs from the rate of increase determined by the biotic
potential. The influence of environmental resistance first appears at this point. In year 8 the
point of highest yield, at which the annual increment is a maximum, is reached; thereafter, as
a result of increasing environmental resistance, the yield decreases.

maximum sustainable yield, a concept that has been used far too
often in fisheries and wildlife management to the detriment of the
animal populations involved. Note also that in this exercise it is
assumed that the carrying capacity is constant, not affected, for
example, by changes in weather or the effects of plant succession,
and not modified by the increasing population. None of these assumptions is ever true for a deer population or any other population of large grazing herbivores.

SOME REAL LIFE PROBLEMS

Exponential Growth

The George Reserve of the University of Michigan is a fenced 1200-acre enclosure into which deer were introduced in 1928. The initial population of 6 deer (2 bucks and 4 does) increased in 6 years to a population of 160. This was considered fantastic at a time when the general public assumed that deer were on their way to extinction. In a paper describing the situation by O'Roke and Hamerstrom (1948) it is pointed out that this increase could only have been achieved by the deer achieving their biotic potential rate of increase throughout the six-year period. If density-dependent environmental resistance had operated, this rate of increase would have shown some decline as the carrying capacity was approached. By the end of seven years, when the population had passed the 200 mark, it was evident that the carrying capacity had been exceeded, and damage to the habitat was obvious. After this time the population was reduced by shooting in the way shown in Figure 7.2, and thereafter the numbers reflect the degree of hunting pressure. (Further adventures of the George Reserve deer herd are reported in papers by Chase and Jenkins, 1962, and Croon, *et al.*, 1968.)

For these deer it must be assumed that maximum natality is achieved and no mortality is experienced until after some threshold point, perhaps representing the carrying capacity of the area, is reached. Of course, in a fenced area, predators were absent. A similar pattern of increase is shown by some mountain sheep populations. Buechner (1960) has analyzed the growth of three mountain sheep populations in Montana: one introduced to Wildhorse Island in Flathead Lake, another in the Fort Peck game range, and a third in the Tarryall Mountains. All these show evidence of increase at a biotic potential rate, unmodified by any density-dependent mortality until such time as the environmental capacity is reached or at least approached closely. It is not unlikely that this represents a typical pattern for large herbivores in areas where predation is absent or limited, and where other environmental conditions are not severe. This kind of population behavior has given rise to another model, the J-shaped curve, which

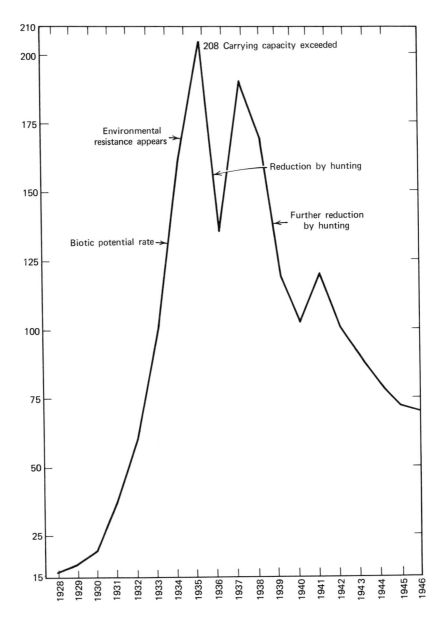

Figure 7.2. Actual curve of population growth and decline in the George Reserve Deer Herd, Michigan.

resembles the George Reserve curve up to the year 1936, or with St. Paul reindeer (Fig. 7.3) up to the year 1940. It represents biotic potential growth without the modifying effect of environmental resistance, a process known as exponential growth.

$$(\Delta N / \Delta t = rN)$$

Slow Growth

The introduction of domesticated reindeer into a previously ungrazed tundra range on the Pribilof Islands, east of mainland Alaska, has provided interesting information about population increase and decline that was reported in a paper by Victor Scheffer (1951) (Fig. 7.3). On the two islands, St. George and St. Paul, where reindeer were liberated, the pattern of growth departed strongly from the logistic model. In both areas, if year by year increase is considered, there is a failure to achieve a biotic potential rate of increase. The initial period of establishment, from 1911 to 1929, is much longer than would be predicted. Since there was no predation or hunting at this time, the cause of this slow rate of increase is not known. After 1929, on St. Paul, the growth curve bends sharply upward, but at no time is the biotic potential

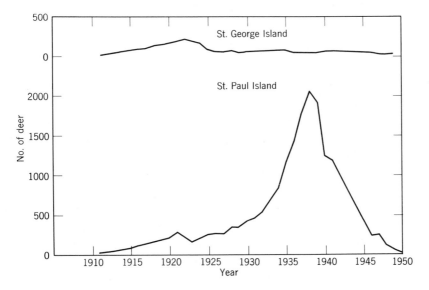

Figure 7.3. Reindeer on Pribilof Islands (Scheffer, 1951).

Domestic reindeer in the USSR. Introduction of this species to the Pribilof Islands brought results that were not anticipated.

growth equalled. Furthermore, there is no density-dependent decrease in the rate of growth as carrying capacity is approached. The carrying capacity for St. Paul allowed 33 acres per reindeer and a total population of 800 animals. However, after this carrying capacity was exceeded, the St. Paul reindeer put on a more rapid spurt of growth than was exhibited during many of the years when numbers were much less. Thereafter, the J-shaped crash sets in, but without any recovery or leveling off. The population goes on down to near extinction. On St. George the reindeer did not succeed at all, although there was some slight initial increase.

In reviewing this situation, it is probably more usual for exotic introductions to fail than for them to succeed. There are too many factors in a new environment to which a species must adjust, and it is not at all easy to determine in advance what will be limiting. Nor is it at all unusual for large exotic herbivores to overshoot carrying capacity, destroy their environment, and go on down to extinction. This has happened to rabbit populations on Midway Island near Hawaii and sheep and goat populations on many Pacific islands where they have been left to a feral existence. Large herbivores do not starve quickly. Unlike shrews, they hang on when food supply is inadequate and can continue to depress the forage plant production.

Failures to increase at rates that closely approach biotic potential are probably more numerous than the reverse. Examples from European Bison in a Polish reserve, and the American Bison in Wood Buffalo National Park are given in the next chapter. There is some evidence, originally advanced by the pioneer animal ecologist W. C. Allee (1931), that too small a population will have reduced success in reproduction, and that for some species at least a threshold must be reached before most females of breeding age begin to produce young. For example, Fraser Darling (1938) found this breeding threshold in populations of sea birds off the coast of Scotland: with too few birds no nesting occurred.

The construction of population models can be fascinating to the mathematically inclined, and extremely useful to all concerned with the ups and downs of animals or plants. Thus far we have looked at two simple examples, diagrammed as S-shaped and J-shaped curves. Many more complicated and realistic models have been worked out. For example, Dean Medin and Allen Anderson carried out a five-year study of mule deer in Larimer County, Colorado, and obtained detailed information on population parameters and habitat characteristics. From this they developed a simulation model of the mule deer population and its environment that could be programmed into a computer. Questions about the effect of different levels of hunting or other changes in environmental factors on both the deer and its habitat could be asked and the computer could produce answers that would otherwise be obtained only through laborious calculations. Although perhaps unduly modest about the usefulness of their results, they have this to say:

It seems to us that simulation models have a potential for guiding selection among alternative images of the future, however dim those images may be. An optimistic view is that simulation models of biological systems can provide valuable management planning aids. At the very least, the explicit nature of simulation models invites critical and constructive thought. Only application and testing will confirm the degree to which this, or any model, has the kind of utility suggested by our final question . . . Can we develop a model that will help decisionmakers identify preferred courses of management action? (Medin and Anderson, 1979)

The student who wishes to pursue this subject further could well begin with Caughley's (1977) *Analysis of vertebrate populations.*

THE ANNUAL CYCLE OF POPULATIONS

Once an animal population has become established in an environment, it is not expected that population fluctuations will cease. Instead, even in those environments with reasonably constant carrying capacity, seasonal changes in animal numbers will take place. In all areas outside the humid tropics, and with some species within the humid tropics, there is a distinct seasonal fluctuation in plant growth (Stubblebine, *et al.,* 1978). In temperate regions the spring is a period of active vegetation growth, followed by a period when flowering and fruit formation occur and then a period during which all production ceases. (In the sub-humid or semi-arid tropics one finds similar periodicity associated with the wet season.) Animals have adapted to these seasonal changes in vegetation through an annual cycle of growth and decrease. The young of most species will be born during a period when food is most abundant, and there is consequently a distinct natality season, of short duration, during which most births or hatchings will take place. Animals born later or earlier than this period may encounter hardships involving shortages in food quantity and quality, and in usual circumstances are less likely to survive.

With any prolific species there can be enormous differences between population densities before and after the breeding season. For some species, particularly upland game birds in stable habitats, the low points of the annual cycle remain quite constant from year to year, and are attained at the start of the breeding season. High points vary with reproductive success and early mortality of young, but the mortality after the breeding season shows, in general, a density dependence that returns the population each year to the same general level. Some consider this annual low point to be a measure of the carrying capacity of the habitat. In theory, it can only be increased if the habitat is improved. Efforts to modify it by attacking the causes of loss during the year often will show little result.

Various studies of game birds have involved the control of two separate decimating factors: predation and hunting. In one of these, carried out with ruffed grouse in Michigan and reported by Palmer, the situation illustrated in Figure 7.4 was observed. Here one grouse population (Gladwin) was completely protected from hunting, whereas the other, in a roughly similar habitat (Rifle River), was exposed to intensive sport shooting, with the result that in one year 52 percent of the fall population was shot. From 1950 to 1955 numbers of grouse were regularly censused in both areas. The pattern of the annual cycle was similar in both. Although there were year-to-year differences, both showed approxi-

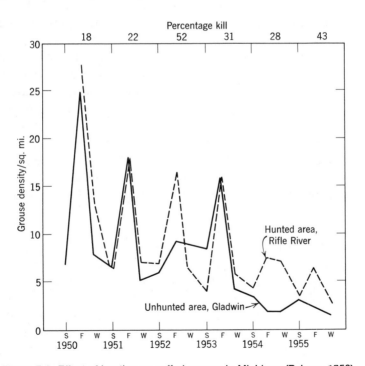

Figure 7.4. Effect of hunting on ruffed grouse in Michigan (Palmer, 1956).

mately the same average spring populations over the six-year period.

An analysis of the results of this Michigan study reveals certain principles that have been demonstrated equally well in a number of other studies. One is that mortality, among these birds, is usually density dependent. The elimination of one decimating factor—hunting—does not increase populations. Instead, other decimating factors operate more strongly to cause roughly the same total mortality. Decimating factors thus tend to operate in a manner that Paul Errington has called *compensatory,* and the presence of one is compensated by the reduced effects of others.

In another study of ruffed grouse, in New York, reported by Edminster (1933), a different decimating factor—predation—was controlled. Here it was found that the area with the most intensive predator control experienced a greater decrease in grouse numbers than the area with a normal predator population. The study indicated not only that grouse did not benefit from predator removal, but that a normal amount of loss to predation seemed to cut down losses from other factors that were at that time bringing about a statewide decrease in grouse populations.

From these studies it has been concluded that close control over single decimating factors does not necessarily increase game bird populations. In a complex environment a population becomes stabilized when the habitat offers security against further loss. Although natality will increase a population above this level each year, mortality will lower it again to this level. Predation, hunting, and other decimating factors cease to be effective against a population that is securely located. To increase population levels above this point, the habitat must be improved.

"Shootable Surplus"

The nature of the annual cycle and the compensatory action of decimating factors has led wildlife managers to the conclusion that any relatively stable population will produce each year a "shootable surplus" represented by the addition of young animals to the population. This surplus represents the excess numbers above the carrying capacity. Since this excess will die sooner or later, it can be argued that it is safe to take it by hunting. It is even argued that not to do so is a "waste of animals." This could be true if a population existed in isolation, or if the only species of any importance to humankind was the species that produced this "surplus." However, since ecosystems are totally interrelated, and all species depend on other species, removal of any significant number of individuals from any population will take them away from other species in that ecosystem that could have eaten them. Hunting, by an outside species that does not form an integral part of an ecosystem, removes the food supply of predators, parasites, scavengers, and all other organisms that are in turn affected by these species. Continued removal of such a "surplus" changes the ecosystem. How much, or in what direction, we have yet to find out. In a highly productive ecosystem, what we choose to call sustained yields can in fact be sustained for a long while. But not without effects on all other species.

Stocking of Game

Consideration of the annual cycle and the control exerted by the habitat on the numbers of animals long ago caused biologists to question the practice, then widespread in game management agencies, of stocking pen-reared game in natural habitats in order to increase populations. If the normal annual increment of young in an area cannot be supported by the habitat, it does not seem reasonable that excess numbers of farm-reared animals added to the population would be supported. Many studies have been carried out to check this idea, and it was found for game birds in particular that an addition of game-farm birds did not increase the breeding population of an area. In fact the survival of game-farm birds was found to be much lower than that of birds naturally produced. Birds released several weeks before a hunting season would usually fail to show up in the hunter's bag, having already died from other causes. Since there was no biological justification for such releases, and the costs of producing game artificially was high, the practice of introducing game-farm birds to improve hunting has been discontinued by most public agencies.

STABILITY OF POPULATIONS

Even in the most unvarying habitat no wildlife population is constant in numbers. There will always be gains from births and losses from deaths. Nevertheless, some species, in some environments, show much more stability than others. No population exhibits the great fluctuations of which it is theoretically capable. D. I. Rasmussen (1941) believed that the deer herd of the Kaibab National Forest increased from 4,000 to 100,000 animals in an 18-year period, before it crashed (Fig. 7.5). If true this would be a remarkable record. But with a biotic potential rate of increase the same initial population could have increased to more than 18 million animals, enough to more than stock the entire western United States during the same period of time.

Aldo Leopold has classified population fluctuations into three categories: populations that remain relatively *stable* in numbers from year to year; populations that are normally stable, but occasionally exhibit an increase to a high peak in numbers, or *irruptive* populations; and finally those that fluctuate at regular intervals from a high peak to a low trough in numbers, the *cyclic* populations.

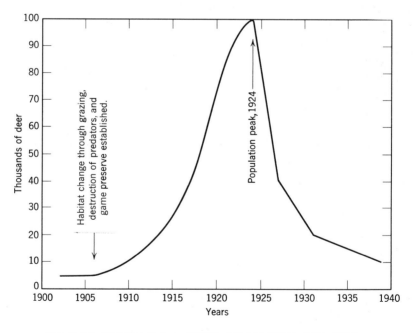

Figure 7.5. Increase in deer, Kaibab, Arizona (Rasmussen, 1941).

Stable Populations

In the more humid ecosystems where temperature and rainfall do not change much from year to year, habitats will remain relatively stable in carrying capacity if not disturbed. In such habitats one would expect to find relatively stable populations, with numbers going up and down in an annual cycle, but returning each year to the same base level. For example, Brewer has pointed out that over a period of 18 years "the number of red-eyed vireos breeding in a 65-acre beech-sugar maple forest near Cleveland, Ohio, studied by A. B. Williams, never went below 18 nor exceeded 36." It is useful to consider this kind of population as a "normal" or standard kind of behavior. Exceptions to it therefore require further investigation and explanation. Often these exceptions, resulting in fluctuations that exceed this normal, will be found to have their cause in habitat disturbance—the destruction of climax and its replacement by successional vegetation. In other instances, fluctuations will be found to stem from changes in weather conditions. However, some categories of fluctuations (notably the cyclic variety) occur in what appear to be stable, climax habitats and show no clear relationship to weather or other obvious environmental changes.

Cyclic Populations

In the far north, the Arctic of North America and Eurasia, lemming populations go up and down in a reasonably regular and predictable manner. These mouselike rodents first hit the news in Scandinavia, where they inhabit the mountains and plateaus. Once in a while they increase to enormous numbers, overrun their natural habitat, and move down mountain through the farmlands, towns, or even cities of the lower country. Such mass movements were bound to attract attention, and in time gave rise to a considerable mythology. When lemmings were observed swimming in the fiords, into which they had perhaps fallen, the story grew that they were striking out into the Atlantic following a long-lost migration route to the vanished continent of Atlantis. Despite this conspicuous behavior, lemmings were regarded by European scientists much as the present day crop regards UFOs or ESP. Serious investigations first took place in America rather than the Scandinavian arctic.

Population studies of lemmings, particularly of the brown lemming (*Lemmus*), revealed that in the American tundra they fluctuate in a fairly regular cycle with peaks usually occurring at three to four year intervals. A similar cycle is found in voles (*Microtus*) in lower latitudes. Tied to this cycle in the arctic and subarctic are those predators that depend on lemmings or voles, the arctic fox, snowy owl, and red fox in particular. When lemmings or voles are abundant, these predators increase to high numbers also. When the rodents crash, the predators have few alternate prey to turn to and must therefore die off, or emigrate. The periodic appearance of snowy owls in the lower 48 states, far from their normal range, is the result of such emigration.

At times the cycles in lemmings or voles appear to be synchronized over broad regions. An example of both the regularity and the degree of synchronization is provided by one of the early studies of the vole cycle, that of the British ecologist, Charles Elton. Elton (1942) investigated the fur returns of red foxes trapped throughout Labrador and turned in to the Moravian missions of that country. When these returns were plotted on a graph, the picture shown in Figure 7.6 was revealed, a cycle with peaks usually at three to four year intervals, but one in which the height of the peaks varied greatly from one time to another. Since the red foxes in Labrador were feeding mostly on voles, their numbers were changing as the numbers of voles changed. It appeared therefore that voles throughout Labrador increased to peaks and subsequently died off at approximately the same time; that the cycles were synchronized in some way.

Moving from Labrador to Scandinavia, it becomes possible to relate the spectacular lemming "plagues" of that region to the irregular occurrence of unusually high peaks in an otherwise regular cycle.

For a long while the four-year cycle was observed, described, but not explained. However, during the 1950s and 1960s various studies were undertaken that have removed much of the mystery from this cycle, while still leaving it as an interesting example of population behavior. One such study is that of Fritz Frank (1957), who investigated populations of the vole, *Microtus arvalis,* in Germany. He relates the cyclic increase of this species to three factors: its biotic potential, the carrying capacity of the habitat, and the

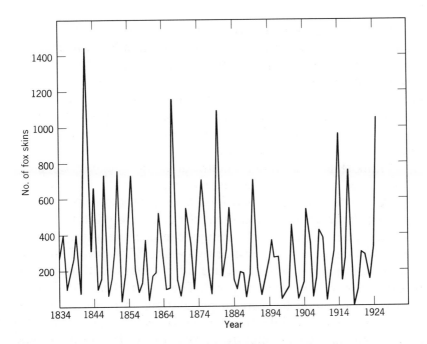

Figure 7.6. Four-year cycle in red fox, based on fur returns from Moravian Missions, Labrador (Elton, 1942).

"condensation potential" of the animals. The biotic potential allows a rapid increase to a high density. Such an increase is not widely expressed, however, unless the species occurs in areas of suitable carrying capacity. In Germany such areas are described as "large, open, monotonous, and uniform biotopes with extremely scant cover of trees and bushes, which we call "cultivation steppes" caused by human activity." In areas of intensive farming or diversified vegetation, cycles do not occur. In suitable areas, however, it it possible for voles to increase simultaneously over a wide region. In these areas the vole exhibits an ability to tolerate crowding, the "condensation potential" that is not characteristic of voles in noncyclic populations, where a form of territorial behavior is more common. In the cyclic areas, however, females form large overwintering groups, and in some instances several females from the same litter will join to rear their young in a common nest. With this condensation potential in operation, there is no behavioral limit on population increase to a high density.

Under these circumstances, with normal natality, a population can increase from a low point to an extremely high level, in excess of the carrying capacity, in a period of three years. At this level, however, the climatic stress of winter, shortage of food, excessive crowding, and conflict between individuals all exert pressures on the voles. This causes a population crash. The immediate cause of the crash is believed by Frank to be a breakdown in the adrenal-pituitary system—shock disease.

Frank states that under a constant climatic regime, the population cycles would follow a three-year periodicity. However, favorable winters with increased food and cover allow for a prolongation of the increase, or maintenance of a high level, for four or even five years. Unfavorable winters can occasionally cut off the population increase at the end of two years. Widespread, unfavorable winter weather would reduce all populations throughout a broad region to the same low point. Thereafter, the normal rate of increase would tend to keep all populations in phase for a time, before local habitat differences allowed separate populations to differ from the general picture of synchrony. However, another unfavorable winter would return all populations once more to another low point and restore the synchrony. Frank's studies appear to have provided answers to most of the questions regarding cycles in *Microtus* in Germany. His populations, however, were not much bothered by predation.

In studies in Alaska, F. A. Pitelka (1957) and his co-workers investigated populations of brown lemmings and found no evidence of shock disease in the crashes that occurred in 1953 and 1956. Instead, at the high point of the cycle, lemmings so far exceeded the carrying capacity of their habitat that they destroyed their protective cover by grazing down the grasses and forbs. When the snow melt occurred in the spring, the lemmings were fully exposed to predation. Great concentrations of avian predators, particularly the pomarine jaeger, a sea bird, but also the snowy owl, moved in to reduce the abundant lemmings to a low level. Following this, the cover could once more regrow. The few survivors therefore found abundant shelter during the following years of population growth.

In Pitelka's study the number of avian predators was not tied to the number of lemmings in any one area, nor were the lemming cycles in adjoining areas in phase with one another. Predators could therefore concentrate on one peak population in one year, and then in a subsequent year shift to another area, where a different population would be at a high point.

These studies, and others, provide a general explanation for the lemming-vole cycle. The timing of cycles is determined by the biotic potential of these small mammals, which allows them to exceed carrying capacity over a broad area in three to four years. After this time an overabundant population will necessarily die off, although the particular cause of the crash may vary from place to place. Widespread synchrony is not a necessary feature of the cycle, but where it does occur it may well be brought about by occasional severe winters that affect broad geographic areas, or by other widespread, unfavorable factors that operate on the lemming-vole environments.

The 10-year Cycle   The periodic abundance and scarcity of hares, lynxes, grouse, muskrats, and other species has not given rise to much folk-lore, but it is very much a factor in life in the subarctic, high mountains of the temperate zone, and the northern areas of the United States. At one time an area may be virtually overrun with snowshoe hares, and lynxes will be frequently seen along with horned owls and other normally scarce predators. At other times the same area will be devoid of easily visible animal life. If we think we fully understand the lemming cycle, we can make no convincing claim for the 10-year cycle of hares and lynxes. Various portions of it have been studied in some detail and general records of the cycle have been kept over long periods. But few scientists seem willing to devote 10 to 20 years of their lives watching a population of hares or grouse go up and down. Graduate students, who do most research, operate on a much shorter cycle. Few want to spend a decade earning a doctor's degree. Game departments could afford long-range studies, but political pressures usually require that they devote attention to immediate issues. Besides, 10 years is too long for most people to remember. Events that happen every 10 years tend to be greeted, in each decade, as some entirely new phenomenon that receives its brief spate of coverage in the newspapers or on television.

The long cycle affects a great number of species. It is most characteristic of the boreal forest, below the tundra where the short cycle holds sway. But it is found also in areas well to the south. The snowshoe hare may be cyclic throughout its range. Many birds, including the northern grouse, and at the northern limits of their ranges, pheasants, partridges, and quail, participate in the cycle. Muskrats also show cyclic effects in behavior and reproduction. There is some evidence from Siivonen, in Finland (Hewitt, 1954), that European grouse are affected. Siivonen, however, has stated that the short cycle is basic to northern Europe, but that high peaks in this cycle occur at roughly 10-year intervals, coinciding with the peaks of the North American cycle. A number of predatory animal species, of which the Canada lynx is representative, follow their prey species in cyclic trends. (Fig. 7.7)

Although synchrony between separate cyclic populations is not precise, it is often sufficiently close to make it appear an important feature of the 10-year cycle. Thus, in recent decades, cyclic peaks in most, if not all populations, have come in years ending in 1, 2, or 3, and cyclic lows in the years ending in 5, 6, or 7. The reverse was true in the nineteenth century. It would seem neces-

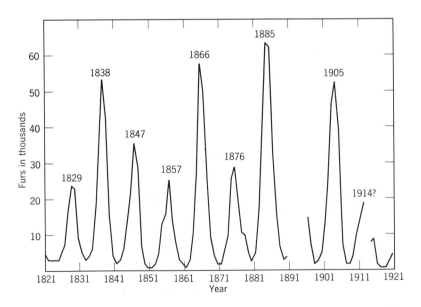

Figure 7.7. The nine-to-ten-year cycle in Canada lynx, from Hudson's Bay Company fur returns (Elton and Nicholson, 1942).

sary to explain why snowshoe hares in Alberta, and the high mountains of West Virginia should both reach a population peak in 1942, the same year in which ruffed grouse were most abundant in Minnesota and Wisconsin, and pheasants in Iowa. In 1951 peaks were recorded for capercaillie, blackgame, and hazel grouse in Finland, corresponding with peaks for Minnesota grouse, snowshoe hares, and other American species. It is to be noted also that not only is a peak in numbers quite widespread in a given two to three year sequence, but also that such features as clutch and litter size and behavior show a similar synchrony over a wide area. Some students of animal populations believe it is necessary to relate this synchrony to some cyclic change in solar radiation or other extraterrestrial influence operating on a worldwide scale, but nobody has really found any that fit.

Some of the first data on North American cycles were presented by Ernest Thompson Seton in his 1923 book *The Arctic Prairies*. Here he presented Hudson Bay Company fur returns showing a 10-year cycle in snowshoe hare and lynx. A study of the lynx fur returns by Elton and Nicholson in 1942 showed an even more remarkable picture of the regularity of the lynx cycle (Fig. 7.7). It was apparent to these investigators that lynx numbers were dependent on numbers of hares, although at times unknown factors caused a decline in lynx abundance while hares were still numerous. Illustrations of some additional studies are presented in Fig. 7.8. These show a high degree of synchrony between peaks and troughs in many areas. However, separate areas may be two to three years apart in the timing of their peaks, suggesting that no single climatic incident is involved.

One of the more interesting accounts of the interactions involving cyclic species has been provided by Arthur Bergerud who has investigated the population dynamics of caribou in Newfoundland. This large island (42,000 sq. mi.) was inhabited by caribou and wolves when it was first settled. Investigations of caribou in the period 1900–1915 indicated that caribou were abundant, with some estimates being as high as 200,000 animals. Bergerud, however, has calculated more realistically that the population at that time was 40,000. Wolves were persecuted by the early pioneers, and in 1911 the last one was reported killed. Starting in 1915 caribou began a rapid and continuing crash to a low level of

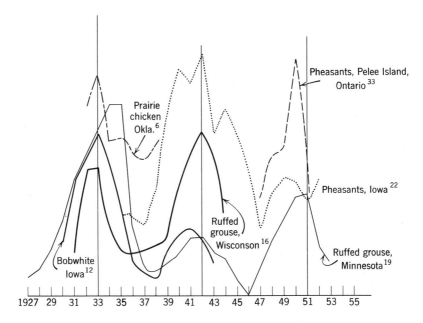

Figure 7.8. The nine-to-ten-year cycle in American game birds (from various sources) (Scales differ with species).

perhaps 2000 animals in 1930. Heavy hunting, perhaps 7000 a year, was the major cause of mortality, but there were other contributing factors.

The Canada lynx may or may not have been originally native to Newfoundland. There is no doubt that it was scarce during the 1800s. The snowshoe hare did not occur in Newfoundland until it was introduced late in the nineteenth century. It then began to increase. "The first high in numbers of hare lasted from 1896 to 1915." According to D. G. Dodds, who studied the hares, this initial peak was the greatest density of hares ever attained on the island. During the increase in hares there was a buildup in lynx, and they became "exceedingly abundant when hares reached high densities." In 1915 the hare population crashed. Lynx were left with few alternative prey to turn to since there are no native forest grouse, and arctic hares and ptarmigan were not sufficiently abundant. Lynx began to prey heavily on caribou calves, and this in combination with heavy human predation prevented caribou from recovering.

Since the 1915 crash, snowshoe hares have become tied to the 10-year cycle, apparently with the usual lows in mid-decade, and highs in the early part of each decade. During the build-up of hares to the 1960-1961 peak, predation by lynx on caribou calves appeared to have declined and calf survival was high. Caribou numbers have also fluctuated between 1930 and 1967, with highs probably reached in 1941, 1951, and 1961, with populations in the middle 1960s being approximately 7500. Other than human hunting, lynx predation on calves appeared to be the principal mortality factor affecting caribou populations. Thus, through extermination of the original key predator—the wolf—and introduction of a new herbivore—the snowshoe hare—caribou populations seem to have become tied to the cyclic fluctuations of what had been originally a minor, if not totally insignificant, predator—the Canada lynx (Bergerud, 1971).

Explanations of the 10-year cycle have been numerous, including Lack's (1934) argument that it is a simple predator-prey interaction; the proposal by Green, Evans, Larson, and others (1939, 1940) that it is tied to the periodic recurrence of overcrowding followed by shock disease; Errington's (1945) evidence that a periodicity in behavior including tolerance to crowding is involved; Grange's (1948) proposal that the cycle is tied to periodic fires and plant succession; or Lamont Cole's view (Hewitt, 1954) that there is simply an interaction of random environmental influences behind the whole thing. It would be pointless to attempt another summary of the now vast amount of literature since this was done in a book by Lloyd Keith in 1962 *(Wildlife's Ten-Year Cycle)*. Keith and his co-workers, however, have now attempted the long-term field studies in Ontario needed to develop a greater understanding of the phenomena involved. Papers by Rusch, *et al.* (1971) and Brand, *et al.* (1976) represent progress reports on these continuing investigations.

Irruptive Populations

An irruption differs from a cycle in its lack of regular periodicity. A population that is usually stable will increase to a high peak and then crash, only to return to a condition of relative stability once more. Figure 7.9, showing the raccoon fur take by the Hudson's Bay Company, illustrates the process. Sometimes the reasons for an irruption are obvious—a marked change in weather bringing an improvement in carrying capacity, followed by a return to less favorable conditions. Sometimes the reasons are obscure.

An early description of such an event has been left to us in the writings of the naturalist and author, W. H. Hudson (1903), who spent much time in the dry pampas of Argentina. In the summers of 1872 and 1873 there were warm temperatures and abundant rainfall in the pampas. Mice increased so greatly that dogs lived on them, domestic fowl killed them, and the sulphur tyrant birds and Guira cuckoos preyed on nothing else. Domestic cats went wild and lived well. Foxes, weasels, and opossums thrived on a diet of mice, and even armadillos fed on them. In the autumn of 1873 great numbers of storks and short-eared owls

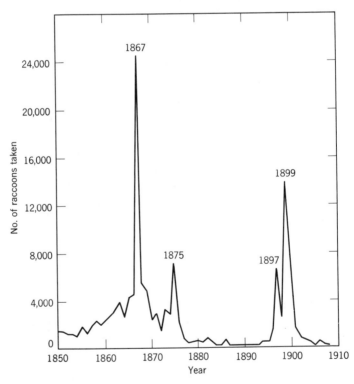

Figure 7.9. Raccoon fur take, Hudson's Bay Company, Canada (Seton, 1923).

joined in the great feast. Owls remained in great numbers into the winter of 1873 and were so well fed that they began to breed in midwinter, so that one nest found in July (midwinter) contained three fat, half-grown young. The winter, however, brought drought. The forage from the preceding summer either had been consumed by cattle and wild game or had dried and disappeared. With the disappearance of both food and cover for the mice, there was a sharp decline in numbers. By late winter in 1873, mice were scarce; short-eared owls moved out of the area, and the burrowing owls, permanent residents, were dying from hunger.

Irruptions in deserts and arid steppes can usually be related to obvious changes in climate. A high rainfall year brings an abundance of vegetation, and quail, chukar partridge, jackrabbits, and other animals can increase. A series of good years brings great abundance. A return to the more usual dry years brings an inevitable population crash. During the dry years game birds may fail to reproduce, eggs may not hatch, or young may be unable to survive. Leopold and others reported in 1976 on one mechanism that inhibits reproduction in quail at such times. A number of plants form compounds similar to animal reproductive hormones. Clover, for example, can contain the equivalent of a heavy dose of diethylstilbestrol (DES)—a hormone that will suppress fertility. Desert annual plants were found by Leopold and company to contain such estrogenic substances during drought years. Quail feeding on them show a marked lowering of fertility.

Among ungulates in the United States, the increase and crash of deer in the Kaibab region of Arizona provides the most frequently quoted example of an irruption. The causes of this can only be surmised, but some marked change in carrying capacity along with freedom from hunting and predation appears to have been involved. The most remarkable feature of this irruption, however, is not its occurrence or its magnitude, but the fact that the same phenomenon has not occurred much more widely, in deer populations exposed to apparently similar conditions.

Among the unexplained and unexplored irruptions, those of the Hudson's Bay Company raccoons are noteworthy (Fig. 7.9), since they occurred in the region of the 10-year cycle but show no correlation with it. For reasons not generally understood, tree squirrels in the Eastern United States occasionally increase to great numbers and then emigrate (Allen, 1943). In the late 1960s thousands of tree squirrels were reported moving down the Appalachian Mountains. I regret to say that I don't know where they were going, or where they ended their long march—at the time biologists appeared to be busy elsewhere.

EVOLUTIONARY STRATEGIES

It may help in understanding the complexity of wildlife population behavior if we consider that wild species have developed, over the course of evolution, strategies that contribute to their survival in the particular kind of habitat to which they are adapted. The word strategy is perhaps misleading since it implies some sort of conscious choice on the part of animals belonging to a particular species, but the word is now well established in the literature (MacArthur and Wilson, 1967), and we will stay with it. Species that are high on the food chain, or have few effective enemies, and that occupy more or less stable environments—the climax of biotic succession—need not for the sake of their survival devote much energy to reproduction and the care and feeding of young. Species of this type tend to have large body size and, if herbivores, exert a strong influence on the vegetation on which they feed or otherwise use. They can increase to high levels of abundance, and must devote a considerable amount of energy to intraspecific interactions, including methods of using their environment that minimize conflict with other members of their own species or species that use the same habitat. Territorial behavior is likely to develop. Specialization in food habits may develop—as, for example, among the ungulates of the African savanna where competition is minimized through each species feeding selectively on particular plants or parts of plants: new leaves, old leaves, stems, twigs, roots, and so on. An advantage accrues to long-lived species, and to slowly maturing species since there is a greater opportunity to learn and pass on information, and rapid reproduction is no advantage when populations have stabilized in a stable environment. Such species that are considered to live near the carrying capacity *(K)* of their environment have been termed *K-selected species* by MacArthur and Wilson. One can think of many examples: musk ox, bison, great whales, elephants, or among car-

California condor. One of the many K-selected species that are now critically endangered.

nivores the grizzly bear, mountain lion, tiger, jaguar, wolf, or with birds the passenger pigeon, ivory-billed woodpecker, pileated woodpecker, condor, whooping crane, sandhill crane, great auk, Emperor penguin. If a number of extinct or threatened species seem to be on this list, it is no coincidence.

At the other extreme are what some have called "animal weeds"; along with plant weeds they occupy marginal or early successional habitats—habitats that are created by disturbance but are ephemeral in nature. Such habitats initially are unstocked and are occupied by pioneers that move into a habitat where resources are temporarily abundant. For such species a rapid rate of reproduction and increase is important, for the species that breeds and spreads the fastest tends to occupy the ground for as long as that ground is available. General instead of specialized feeding habits are an advantage, to benefit from the variety of pioneer plants. A high dispersal ability is important since areas of new disturbance will appear as the old ones close over and disappear. Small size helps, since most energy can be devoted to reproduction rather than extended growth. Elaborate mechanisms for avoiding or minimizing conflicts with other members of the same species or of potential competitors are less advantageous than the capacity to outbreed them. Species that follow this general pattern are those that emphasize a maximum potential rate of increase *(r)*, and are known as *r-selected species*. Examples again readily come to mind: white-footed mice, voles, lemmings, hares, jackrabbits, quail, grouse, house rats, most flocking birds that occupy weedy ground (starlings, Brewer blackbirds, cowbirds, house sparrows, etc.). If these again seem familiar as the species that are involved in cycles, irruptions, and similar "explosive" population phenomena, that also is no coincidence. The list also contains the species with which wildlife managers have credited themselves with the greatest success in their efforts at wildlife restoration. It also contains the world's most outstanding pests.

The distinction between *K*- and *r*-selected species is obviously very important for wildlife management. For example, Miller and Botkin at Yale have developed computer models for various *K*-selected species. When the stated hunting take of sandhill crane was related to the total population of that species, the model predicted that this harvest, amounting to only 6 percent of the population, would result in extinction after 19 years, something that would not have been predicted from common sense or from "rule of thumb" estimates. I regret to say, however, that the information fed to the computer was wrong—the hunting take, in fact, was considerably less than 6 percent (Ripley and Lovejoy, 1978). The point of this exercise is, however, that you cannot expect rapid bounce-back from *K*-selected species subject to harvesting by hunting, fishing, trapping, or other means. They may simply become extinct. By contrast, it is often extremely difficult to control *r*-selected species—and in this category are most of our "pest" insects against which we have waged a pesticide war that makes very little ecological sense.

8

LEVELLING OFF

THE MANY MEANINGS OF CARRYING CAPACITY

It is by now obvious, or should be, that any habitat can support only a limited number of animals and that population increase above this limit cannot be sustained. Thus far I have used the term carrying capacity to mean this limitation imposed by the environment. Carrying capacity is considered a function of the habitat, rather than of factors intrinsic to the animal population. Aldo Leopold used the term in this sense in his classic *Game Management,* although, perhaps wisely, he did not clearly define it. The general usage of the term along with the lack of a clear definition of its meaning has been discussed in a review paper by Edwards and Fowle (1955). Although these authors take a step toward clarifying the meaning of carrying capacity, a considerable area of confusion is left, ready to trap the unwary student of populations, and to baffle the interested public.

Three important ways in which "carrying capacity" has been used are: (1) the number of animals of a given species that are actually supported by a habitat, measured over a period of years; (2) the upper limit of population growth in a habitat, above which no further increase can be sustained; and (3) the number of animals that a habitat can maintain in a healthy, vigorous condition.

In the first sense, the term carrying capacity is used for most bird populations. In examples given earlier, where single decimating factors—hunting or predation—were eliminated, the population levelled off at about the same point each year. This level, reached by a population at the low point of its annual cycle, was considered the carrying capacity. What factors actually determined the level were not examined. The implication behind this usage is that a population at this level is relatively *secure,* and unlikely to undergo much further loss from decimating factors.

The second meaning of the term is usually in connection with the sigmoid curve of population growth. It is the upper limit, the levelling-off point where natality equals mortality. It is assumed in the logistic model that mortality will start, or natality will decrease, well before this K level is reached. The K level is the balance between biotic potential and environmental resistance. It is significant that populations below this K level are not *secure* in any sense, but are subjected to mortality that increases in intensity with population density. Shortages of food, cover, and shelter at levels below K contribute to the increasing mortality.

The third sense in which carrying capacity is used is borrowed largely from range management and animal husbandry and has been expressed by Humbert and W. Dasmann (1945). Since present day livestock owners prefer to have each of their animals in the best of condition, and not exposed to unnecessary hardship, it is implicit that a population at carrying capacity will have sufficient food and shelter, that its natality will not be impaired, and that it will undergo no mortality from malnutrition, diseases, or other obvious causes. A population at this level is healthy and vigorous. The level is definitely not the K level and more closely resembles the MSY point on the logistic curve.

It is too late to do anything about the many meanings of carrying capacity, except to realize that they exist and to live with them. We will therefore go on to examine some definitions of levels that may prove to be more useful, or help to focus thinking about populations.

Subsistence Density

The first level to be considered is the K level, the upper limit at which a population can be sustained, which is determined usually by the ability of the habitat to provide food for support of the population. This is determined, for herbivores, by the primary productivity of the vegetation, and for carnivores by primary productivity processed through the secondary productivity of the herbivores. A population living at or near a subsistence level can obtain enough food for survival, but not necessarily enough for good health, optimum growth, vigor, or fecundity. It is essentially a potential disaster level that can fluctuate with small changes in weather or the seasonal cycle of growth and dormancy in plants. Any unfavorable change can cause widespread decimation. In the absence of such disasters, populations can hang on for a long time at a subsistence density. Natality is rigorously balanced by mortality, fluctuating a bit with good years or poor. Productivity is generally low.

An example of a population living at or near a subsistence level is provided by the Devil's Garden mule deer herd of northern California (Fig. 8.1). Population studies in this area were begun in 1938 and have continued. Salwasser (1979) has projected their numbers back to 1880 to provide nearly 100 years of information. The deer migrate from the Fremont National Forest of Oregon for distances up to 100 miles to a winter range in Modoc County, California. Here they join with various smaller herds, resident in California, to exert a high degree of grazing and browsing pressure on an arid sagebrush and juniper winter range in the Devil's Garden. Salwasser has indicated that favorable conditions for deer were created by timber cutting, heavy livestock grazing, and other disturbance before the 1920s. With essentially new successional habitat the deer went into an irruptive, or exponential, increase in the 1920s and 1930s to reach a peak population in 1940 of perhaps 30,000 animals. Then there was the predictable crash with a loss down to roughly 13,000 during several years, then ups and downs mostly between 15,000 and 25,000 until the late 1960s. After that the population began a rapid, continuing collapse to a level around 8,000 in the late 1970s. Ironically enough after a long period of severely limited hunting, taking only older males, the California Department of Fish and Game managed in the late 1950s to have a realistic either-sex hunt in the area of the Devil's Garden herd. Although the total kill could have little lasting effect on the population, local people were convinced that "doe shoot-

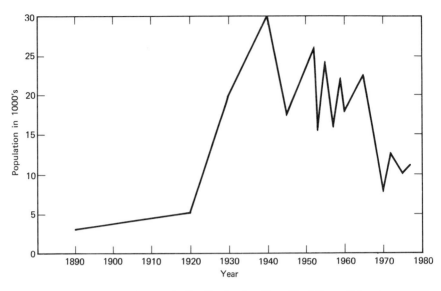

Figure 8.1. Population changes in Devil's Garden Deer Herd (from Salwasser, 1979).

ing" finished off the deer herd. With the help of the state legislature they managed to prevent any further efforts at "deer management."

Range studies in the Devil's Garden showed in the 1950s that severe browsing pressure was being exerted on shrubs, and that bitterbrush, regarded as a key plant for winter survival of deer, was overused. Some shrubs were being killed, and little or no replacement was taking place. During the 1940s, 1950s, and early 1960s the fluctuations of the deer herd were marked by severe winter losses, depressed natality, low post-natal survival, and an unbalanced sex ratio. Body size and antler quality deteriorated. Finally, with successional processes in operation, forests were growing up and closing over on the summer range, and shrubs were being replaced by grasses on the rest. Deer are still at a subsistence level, but this level continues downward. Wildlife biologists should gain merit for having predicted all this, but no badges are being awarded. It is still impossible to manage either population levels or to improve habitat substantially because of political pressures.

Optimum Density

A second level at which a population can be stabilized is an optimum density, a term equivalent to the usage of the term carrying capacity in range management. A population at this level has adequate food, water, and other necessities to meet its needs. Mortality as a result of shortages in the habitat will be minimized, except where severe weather or other temporary factors bring drastic changes in the habitat. Such a population is not immune to predation, but losses will usually not be excessive. Body size, health, growth, and fecundity will approach the maximum for the species. Productivity will be high. However, since essentially no factor is limiting, this is not a point at which a population will level off, unless it is held there by predation, human hunting, or where the behavior of the animals through some form of territoriality prevents any further increase.

Virtually all populations reach this optimum density, but it is difficult to find examples of any that hold themselves or are held at this level. We will examine some possibilities in the next two sections.

Security Density

A level at which a population is held normally through the operation of hunting or predation (hunting being a form of predation) is termed a security density. The term is borrowed from and corresponds with Paul Errington's "threshold of security" that he thus describes: "Except in the event of emergencies, populations living below threshold values wintered with slight reduction through predation and self-adjustment. If exceeding thresholds, populations betrayed instability and pronounced vulnerability to predation until again reduced to secure levels." At a given level of predation, the security density is determined by the distribution of escape cover relative to food and other needs. Admittedly, unusual concentrations of predators, or persistent, year-long hunting can depress a population below a security density. Also, some species have no security level against certain kinds of predators. For example, island species that have evolved in the absence of predators often are wiped out when exposed to introduced predators. Colonial nesting birds and breeding colonies of marine mammals may have no protection against human predation. Herding ungulates of the open plains are highly vulnerable to mechanized, modern hunting. Migratory waterfowl, which must concentrate on limited areas of wetland, may have no security density against hunters. But these are not usual. Most wildlife populations have adapted to the presence of their usual predators, and are not easily depleted by regulated sport hunting.

Security and optimum density may sometimes correspond, since predation or hunting are the factors most likely to hold a population at an optimum level. There is, however, no necessary relationship between the two.

In Adolph Murie's classic study of the wolves of Mount Mc-Kinley National Park in Alaska he found that wolf predation was holding the Dall sheep population at a level below that which it had attained during a period when wolves were scarce or absent. Murie believed that the food supply was adequate for this reduced population of sheep, which presumably was somewhere near the optimum level for the habitat. During the time when wolves were scarce, sheep had increased to a high level and subsequently had died off during a severe winter. Disease was present and caused some mortality, whereas lamb production or survival was less than might have been expected (Murie, 1944).

A.W.F. Banfield (1954) has reported that the caribou population of the Canadian tundra was held in check by the combined effects of hunting and wolf predation. The principal loss was to native American hunters, Eskimo and Indian, who depend on caribou for their meat supply. Wolves were a secondary predator. Together the two caused losses that nearly balanced the gains from natality. When other minor losses from accidents, weather, and occasional disease are added in, the total mortality was found to exceed the natality and the herds were decreasing. The caribou were relatively healthy and productive. However, if they were not kept well below a subsistence level, the caribou could seriously damage the fragile lichen habitat at the northern edge of the boreal forest where they winter. This habitat has already been much reduced by fires that have burned during the past half century. Were the lichen range to be damaged by overgrazing, the caribou could follow the pattern of crashing to near extinction exhibited so dramatically by the reindeer of the Pribilofs.

Moose. Studies of moose–wolf relationships support the concept of security density—
a relatively stable balance between predator and prey.

One of the most thoroughly studied populations of large herbivores and their predators is that of Isle Royale in Lake Superior.
In this national park Durward Allen and his colleagues including
L. David Mech and Rolf O. Peterson have carried out studies of
moose-wolf relationships over many years. Moose have occupied
Isle Royale since some reached the island from the mainland early
in this century. For some decades the moose population was free
from predation. Early studies by Murie, Hickie, and Krefting
showed that moose increased to high population levels, perhaps
3000 animals at their highest peak, overgrazed their habitat drastically and suffered from severe die-offs. When wolves first reached
the island, around 1949, the situation changed. The wolf population increased to a level where it controlled the moose population.
In David Mech's words: "since the wolves arrived, moose numbers have been lower than they were previously, the herd has re-

mained relatively stable, and the browse has begun to recover."
An average of 23 wolves kill around 140 calves and 83 adults
annually, a number approximately equal to the annual production
of young (Mech, 1970).

Although Mech and Peterson (1977) provide further examples of wolves controlling large ungulate populations, there are
other examples to the contrary, and one cannot necessarily look to
predation to control the numbers of large mammals. In African
national parks increases of ungulates to levels exceeding the carrying capacity of their habitats are not infrequent, despite the presence of lions, leopards, cheetahs, hyaenas, hunting dogs, and
smaller carnivores. Sometimes control is exercised and one could
perhaps identify a "security density" but this is not consistent nor
universal. The concept of security density appears most applicable
to those species of game occupying habitats where an abundance
and variety of escape cover and shelter, located near food and
water, make it difficult for predators of hunters to do more than
remove excess numbers from the population.

Tolerance Density

A fourth level at which populations may be stabilized was
originally termed the "saturation point" or "saturation density" by
Aldo Leopold (1933). The word saturation, however, suggests a
crowded habitat, or subsistence density, and hence the term tolerance density has been substituted for it here.

A tolerance density level is one above which intraspecific tolerance normally permits no further increase. It is most marked in
territorial species where crowding is prevented by territorial spacing and where populations are checked in their growth through
dispersal brought about by territorial antagonism. Essentially,
space is the limiting factor, as it is related to the degree of crowding that animals will tolerate, but this is influenced in turn by the
availability of food and shelter.

There would appear to be an evolutionary advantage to a
species with a tolerance density equivalent to an optimum density,
so that self-regulation of numbers provides the best conditions for
the breeding population. With nonterritorial species, however, a
tolerance density may be exhibited that is closer to its subsistence
density.

Calhoun, in a review of his studies of the behavior of the Norway rat, has shown that this species exhibits a tolerance density. As we have noted earlier, even in the presence of abundant food and shelter, captive populations did not increase above a level determined by their limited tolerance for one another. This was far below the subsistence level determined by food and shelter, but judging from the aberrant behavior of the rats and the interferences with reproduction, it was well above an optimum density.

In Frank's studies of vole cycles in Germany he noted that a tolerance density normally kept vole populations at some stable level. In cyclic situations, however, this tolerance density seemed to disappear, populations increased to subsistence densities or higher, and subsequently crashed.

An example of a species that exhibits a tolerance density is provided in a report by J. Andersen (1953) on roe deer in Denmark, and in a subsequent study by B. H. Strandgaard (1972). On the Kalø research farm, 213 roe deer were found by Andersen to be living in an area of 2500 acres. The entire population, except for a few survivors, was exterminated by shooting, and the individuals then examined to determine the population characteristics. This unique way of getting an entire population "in hand" is one not normally recommended to wildlife researchers, but the purpose of the Denmark shoot was to restock the woods with a different genetic strain of deer. In the later study, Strandgaard individually captured and tagged from 93 to 97 percent of the population.

It was found that the Kalø roe deer had a high natality rate, near the maximum for the species, and excellent survival of fawns. Mortality was low before the shoot and brought about mostly by a small amount of sport hunting. There was no evidence of any pressure on the food supply, and no indication that a lack of food or cover was experienced by the animals. Population stability was maintained by territorial behavior that caused a dispersal of the excess animals each year. Males had a lower tolerance density than females, with the result that the population had a higher percentage of females, although the sexes at birth were equal (Fig. 8.2).

In other areas of Denmark, where dispersal of roe deer was prevented by the fencing of roe deer woods, excess numbers built

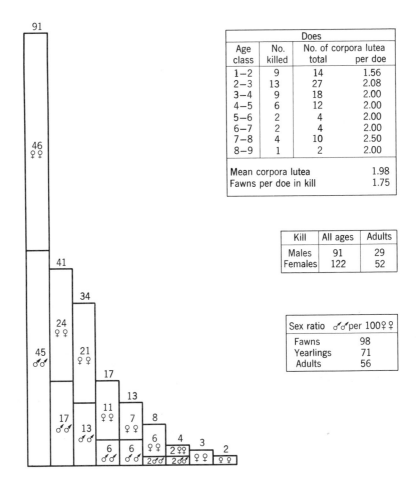

Figure 8.2. Sex and age distribution in 213 roe-deer killed at Kalø, Denmark, 1950 (Anderson, 1953).

up. In these circumstances, evidence of overbrowsing was found, and deer died during the winters from apparent malnutrition. Natality and the physical condition of the confined deer were impaired, whereas the deer existing at a tolerance density were healthy.

Strandgaard's later study, covering the period 1965–1968 was confined to a smaller area of 400 ha. or 1000 acres, from which 107 of Andersen's original animals had been taken. Strandgaard found the population approximately stable at 100 animals (ranging from 92 to 112). However, he points out that dispersal operates effectively at Kalø because of the very intensive roe deer shooting that takes place in Denmark. Dispersing deer can usually find a territory vacated when its previous occupant had been shot. If all woods surrounding Kalø had been fully stocked, deer dispersing into Kalø might have balanced the numbers dispersing outward. Although these animals would be transient, they would in passing exert pressure on food supply, and overpopulation could result. Strandgaard points out that there are reports of overpopulation in Germany, where shooting pressure is more restricted.

Tolerance density levels can be expected to operate in all territorial species. Mech has noted that wolf populations on Isle Royale are stable, fluctuating between 20 and 28 over an eight-year period. Merriam (1964) reported similar stability on Coronation Island in Alaska, whereas Pimlott found a similar situation with a stable density of about one wolf to 10 square miles in Algonquin Provincial Park in Ontario (Mech, 1970). Various instances of relative stability among territorial bird populations have previously been mentioned.

Intermediate Situations

Neat and tidy results are seldom found in natural populations of wild animals, and it is not surprising that many populations fail to fall into such categories. An example is provided by a herd of European bison, which was the subject of observation for many years. This is contrasted with more recent studies of the American bison.

Opportunities to study bison in the wild, when they roamed in their millions over the North American plains, vanished before the science of animal ecology came into existence. In Europe, wild, unconfined herds of bison disappeared at an even earlier date. The European bison was essentially a forest animal, and it is likely that forest, interspersed with glades or meadows, was the original habitat of both surviving bison species.

In the Bialowicza Reserve in Poland, the last wild herd of bison in Europe was long preserved. The reserve was first established in 1803. Population figures are available from 1828 to 1894 (Lydekker, 1898). It has been pointed out that these are very approximate, but they give a useful picture (Fig. 8.3).

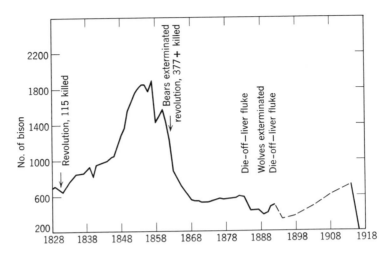

Figure 8.3. Number of bison in Bialowicza Forest, Poland (Lydekyer, 1898; Boyle, 1961).

For nearly thirty years the European bison showed a slow rate of increase, with the percentage of calves in the herd averaging about 7 (4 to 11). Despite the gain in numbers from 700 to 1900, the herd could not be described as productive. Productive herds in America, reported by Fuller, have an annual increment of 27 to 30 percent, instead of 7. In these cows calve every year. In Bialowicza, cows bred only once in three years. Were it not for the steady increase in numbers, one would speculate that the herd was maintained at a subsistence level, and was suffering from its effects. But at a level of 700 they were not noticeably better off than at 1700.

Following the initial increase, the bison experienced a massive die-off, in which their numbers fell from 1900 to 550 over the decade 1858–1868. Although it is probable that this die-off would have occurred in any event, the record is confused by a political revolution that broke out during this period. During the turmoil, poaching may have removed hundreds. After the crash, no increase took place, although hunting had ceased and predation was never important. One could say that the herd stabilized at a new "subsistence level." However in 1884 a new die-off further reduced the population to 380. They fluctuated for a time, and then died off again in 1892–1893. During this period parasitic infections of liver fluke were reported. From the low point of the 1890s, the herd built up to a reported 727 animals in 1914. What might have happened thereafter we cannot know. The entire herd was wiped out when the German and Russian armies clashed in this area in World War I.

During the history of the herd, adult bison seemed almost invulnerable to loss except during the major die-offs. In most years the changes in adult numbers could be attributed to old age. Stability, or slow increase, was a result of extremely low natality and probably mortality of young calves.

Boyle (1961) has reported that food was inadequate for the bison. Although they were fed hay, the nutritional quality of the available food was low. In addition to bison, the area supported many deer that competed for any protein-rich or succulent browse. Qualitative deficiencies in food perhaps allowed adults to survive, but were inadequate for normal reproduction or survival of young. The herd could increase in most years, but was vulnerable to any unfavorable condition. Food was sufficient perhaps in quantity, but lacked all the necessities for balanced nutrition.

The European bison are back at Bialowicza now. A new population was built up from the few animals that had been preserved in zoos. These escaped extermination in World War II and are presently being cared for by Polish and Russian national park managers.

The last large herd of wild bison in North America is in Wood Buffalo National Park in Canada. The Wood Buffalo herd has a history similar to that of Bialowicza. They increased from 1893 to 1922 from 500 to 1500 animals, with an annual percentage of increase similar to the European herd. However, where the European herd crashed after 30 years, the American herd continued to increase—reaching a peak of 12,000 animals in 1934. Part of this increase, however, was caused by the introduction of several thousand plains bison from the south. The original herd is believed to have continued its 7 percent annual gain. Since 1934, the population has remained relatively stable at around 12,000 animals.

Fuller (1962) was of the opinion that the Wood Buffalo herd is being maintained well within the carrying capacity of its habitat. He did not investigate qualitative nutrition. However, stability is maintained partly by tuberculosis, the major cause of mortality, combined with wolf predation. Natality is reduced by brucellosis or contagious abortion. Both diseases are thought to have been absent in the original herd, but were brought in with the plains bison.

Although the Wood Buffalo herd may not exist at a subsistence level, its density is hardly optimum for health or productivity. Under the existing conditions, however, is it more desirable to maintain a stable, not too healthy, not too productive herd? It lives in a national park where hunting is not permitted. A healthy productive herd could present a serious management problem unless predation can build up to a controlling level, and in Wood Buffalo this would depend on the abundance of wolves.

The situation in Yellowstone National Park (Meagher, 1973) also reveals a less than productive herd, or herds, since there are several different populations. There is a relative stability brought about by reduced natality combined with mortality believed to be primarily "winter kill," a result of malnutrition and starvation in times of severe winter weather. Disease is not an important decimating factor. Brucellosis appears to be endemic, but is reported to have no affect on natality; the populations have developed immunity. Some populations appear to be at a subsistence level, others may be somewhat below that. Predation is not significant because of the near extermination of wolves and cougars, and hunting is not permitted. Perhaps it would be possible by range improvement and regulation of herd numbers through shooting to create a much more productive and healthy population. Such an effort, however, would hardly make sense when there is no reason to encourage high productivity. An increase in predator numbers could provide an answer.

A final example will perhaps firmly establish that wildlife populations are often confusing, and sometimes totally confusing. One of the most annoying populations to one who would prefer neat, categorical situations is a population of white-tailed deer reported on by Woolf and Harder (1979) after several years of study. These investigators did all the right things—but the deer show few of the expected characteristics. The population lives in the 2104 ha. (or 5260 acre) Rachelwood Preserve in Pennsylvania. Approximately 1000 deer lived there in 1970, perhaps more, and such a high population was supported over a number of years.

This density of 125 deer per square mile, sustained, would be regarded as unusually high anywhere. The deer, however, were fed supplementarily, with a diet that contained all the right things it was hoped. They were generally healthy. But they were smaller and not so rapidly maturing as uncared for wild deer in nearby areas, outside the fence. Judging from weight and physical characteristics they would appear undernourished. Their reproductive performance was low in all age classes. However, there was little parasitic infection and no serious disease problems. The most frequent disease (enterotoxemia) seemed to result from overeating. Perhaps they were stressed and suffering from shock symptoms? They showed no such evidence. The deer were hunted, or otherwise cropped, with an annual removal from the population of nearly 29 percent, generally considered a high harvest rate. Why weren't they vigorous and productive? We really don't know. Perhaps we can conclude that excessive management of wildlife does not always bring the expected benefits. Certainly our knowledge of populations and ecosystems is still inadequate.

9

DECLINING DIVERSITY

It is not uncommon for people who have been in the wildlife management business to list the successes that have been achieved over the years. There is little doubt that in North America, north of the Rio Grande, and in Europe and the Soviet Union, Australia and New Zealand, South Africa, and a few other places, there have been some great success stories. Thomas Kimball and Raymond Johnson point out that:

> The restoration of certain species is being achieved. Since the early 1930's the number of Pronghorns has increased from 13,000 to about 500,000, Bison from 800 to 6,000, Elk from 41,000 to 1 million, and Whitetail Deer from 350,000 to 12 million; Wild Turkey now live in 43 states, which is more than their natural range encompassed. . . . Northern Fur Seals in Alaska have increased from 215,000 in 1911 up to 1.5 million today, in spite of an annual harvest. The Sea Otter is up to 50,000, its range being restored south to Oregon and Washington, and many individuals are at home again in the kelp beds of the California coast.
>
> The Trumpeter Swans, at a low point in 1935, now number in the thousands. The Wood Duck has recovered from being a nearly endangered species to becoming the most common duck in the southeastern states. Whooping cranes have come up from 14 in the early 1940's to almost 100

today, counting birds in captivity and in the wild. Among mammals, the public attitudes are changing toward the Grey Wolf and Mountain Lion. Once considered predatory villains, they are more widely regarded as desirable and necessary parts of natural ecosystems, and they may be more numerous than were believed 10 years ago.

All this is true, and more, yet few people who are concerned with wildlife conservation are inclined to rest with these past triumphs. In too many areas we are losing ground.

The United States has developed wildlife conservation to a science and art, but in most countries of the world little is known and less is being done to maintain wildlife. Even in the United States and Canada, efforts at protecting threatened species are not necessarily successful. Dwindling numbers of wild animals and increasing likelihood of widespread extinctions are now a worldwide phenomenon.

Dillon Ripley and Thomas Lovejoy (1978) have stated:

That extinction is a natural phenomenon is sometimes advanced as an excuse for not trying to rescue endangered species. This is, of course, nonsensical because although natural extinction is very gradual, occurring over many millenia, today there is considerable additional extinction caused by human interference, so that extinction has become primarily an unnatural phenomenon. . . . In a reasonable stable biosphere the evolutionary rate and extinction rate are approximately equal, and extinction is normally linked with (if not caused by) replacement by a new species. . . . The extinction rate is such today that it is no longer unreasonable to think of a large fraction of the earth's biota becoming extinct before the end of the century.

Extinction occurs when natality fails to keep up with mortality. It can happen suddenly, as with the butchery of an entire population by human hunters—the fate that overtook the Great Auk—but more usually it takes place slowly, a gradual dwindling away of populations such as has been happening up to 1979 with the California condor. It can be caused by habitat destruction, which increases mortality and reduces natality; or by excess killing by humans; or by competition or predation becoming overwhelming; or by outbreaks of usually new diseases or parasitic infestations. It could be caused naturally by hurricanes, volcanic eruptions or similar natural phenomena. Frequently, it is a combination of several of these influences—a habitat is gradually destroyed, the population is forced to live in smaller areas of suitable habitat, and the decreased numbers become increasingly vulnerable to death from a variety of proximate causes.

SPECIES EXTINCTION AND AREA SIZE

John Terborgh and Blair Winter have discussed some of the causes of extinction in a 1979 paper. They find that "The most far-reaching result of past studies is the demonstration that extinction is strongly area dependent, as anticipated by island biogeographic theory." The theory referred to was originally advanced by MacArthur and Wilson (1967) when they examined the numbers of species occurring on islands, compared to those occupying comparable areas of mainland. Species numbers decreased with size of island and with distance of the island from the mainland. At a constant distance from the mainland, larger islands would support a greater number of species. Among islands of comparable size, species numbers decreased with distance from mainland. Two principal factors were involved in this phenomenon: the rate of colonization and establishment, which added new species to the island, and the rate of extinction which removed species. At an equal distance from the mainland, opportunities for colonization would be equal for large and small islands. Differences in species numbers would result from more rapid extinction rates on small islands. This earlier theory has been examined by many investigators. It has been found, for example, by Diamond, (1972) that on land bridge islands, which at the time of their isolation from the mainland (e.g., by rising sea levels following glaciation) could be expected to have the same complement of species as comparable mainland areas, the numbers of species decrease until an equilibrium is reached. This equilibrium level will be higher on large islands, and decline more or less in direct proportion to island size. The immediate cause of extinction seems less important than the fact that extinction will occur, for one reason or another, in small isolated areas. Further evidence is provided by Barro Colorado Island, created when the Panama Canal was built and Gatun Lake flooded as a result of the canal's construction. Barro Colorado has been a strict nature reserve, maintained and carefully protected by the Smithsonian Institution, and intensively studied by biologists. Despite this, it has lost species at a rate comparable to any other land-bridge island. "Birds, reptiles and mammals are included in the list of species that have disappeared. Because of Barro Colorado's status as a research preserve, the extinctions have been carefully documented, not just presumed (Willis, 1974). In spite of this, the underlying causes remain a mystery."

The apparent fact that species will become extinct if they are isolated in small areas is of major concern to those who hope to preserve the world's biota in national parks and reserves, while allowing areas surrounding these reserves to be used for intensive production of things that people may want or need. The largest of existing national parks and reserves is probably not big enough to support a full complement of species—with some exceptions such as the 70 million hectare North Greenland National Park that supported very few species to begin with.

However, it is not enough to know that species will become extinct in small isolated areas; we need also to understand why. Again Terborgh and Winter (1979) have advanced some possible reasons. Among bird families occurring on land-bridge islands they find that falcons, pheasants, woodpeckers, babblers, tinamous, guans, hornbills, and toucans are apparently extinction prone, whereas pigeons, cuckoos, swifts, kingfishers, thrushes, and Old-World warblers *(Sylviidae)* are resistant to extinction. Among the extinction prone are large-bodied, fruit-eating birds. Body size, in itself, does not appear to be directly related to extinction—although one can think of the moas, dodos, auk, which are extinct, and others such as the condors, and several other large raptors, which are endangered. Willis' (1978) studies in Brazil led him to the conclusion that large fruit-eating birds, large raptors, and large terrestrial insect-eating birds are particularly extinction prone. Terborgh and Winter find that birds that normally exist at low population densities are likely to become extinct.

On Barro Colorado island, Terborgh and Winter offer the possibility that disappearance of top predators from an ecosystem can cause drastic reorganization and simplification among the survivors. On Barro Colorado, the normally occurring top predators—jaguar, cougar, and harpy eagle—vanished decades ago. As a result, medium-sized to large mammals such as peccaries, monkeys, and coatis have become unusually abundant. These prey on the eggs and nestlings of ground-dwelling birds. Of the 15 to 18 species of forest birds that have recently become extinct within the reserve, most are ground-nesting species or species that nest near the ground and are thus vulnerable to predation by these abundant mammals. None of these cause-and-effect relationships can be proved on Barro Colorado since the species that could provide the answers no longer exist there. They could be investigated in other areas where the species still survive. Consideration of this makes one wonder what actually did happen to the North American fauna when wolves, grizzly bears, and other top predators were knocked out of the picture. Nobody carried out the studies necessary to give the answers, but we may still be living with some of the reverberations.

DESTRUCTION OF HABITAT

Probably the greatest area of concern for species populations lies in the massive destruction of habitat that is now taking place worldwide. The worst situation appears to be in the humid tropics that represent the world's greatest reservoir of terrestrial animal and plant species. Species diversity in tropical humid forests is almost inconceivable to those familiar only with the temperate zone. For some examples: Frank Golley counted the number of tree species in a plot 5 meters wide by 50 meters long. One hundred and twenty species, more than occur in Great Britain, were found on this single plot (Shane, 1978). Not all humid tropical forest plots would be equally diversified, but the total species diversity is enormous. The vegetation diversity is related to diversity in animal life. Most of the world's bird species and a great variety of mammals, reptiles, and amphibians live in the humid tropics. It has been estimated that half the terrestrial species of plants and animals belong to the humid tropical forests of Latin America, Southeastern Asia, the Pacific Islands, and central and western Africa. The original area of humid forests in the tropics (before European impact) is believed to be 1600 million hectares (4000 million acres). Forty percent of that had been eliminated by 1978. There were in 1978, 935 million hectares remaining in actual forest, and this was estimated to be disappearing at a rate of 110,000 square kilometers per year. This area being decimated each year (around 42,000 sq. mi.) is more than the area of all national forests and national parks in California. This loss of tropical forests is without precedent. It is not as though the forests had simply been cut over and allowed to regrow. In most instances they are cleared, more or less permanently, for agriculture, grazing, or plantations of rapidly growing, single-species stands of exotic trees. According to Barney (Shane, 1978), reporting on the Global 2000 evaluation of the earth's resources conducted by the federal Council of Environmental Quality:

> *Given the amount of original tropical forest already lost and the estimate of an additional two-thirds loss of the remainder by 2000, it seems that tropical forest diversity and the number of species in the* remaining tropical forests *will have been reduced by one half. It has been estimated that 10 percent of the world's biota is dependent on virgin Amazonia forest, five percent on the less diverse and less widespread African forest, and 10 percent on Southeast Asian forest, thus the diversity loss* worldwide *from removal of two-thirds of the tropical forests (alone) would amount to one-eighth of the planet's biota.*

With loss of tropical rainforest, the species that depend on it will also disappear. This gorilla in Zaire is one of thousands of species now threatened by rainforest destruction.

The changes in tropical forests are certainly the most devastating changes now going on, but they are not the only catastrophic decline in wildlife habitat. Some 43 percent of the earth's land surface is already desert or semi-desert. A further 19 percent (30 million sq. km) is now threatened with desertification, according to studies carried out for the United Nations. This threatened area alone is about three times the size of the United States. The world's drylands are being degraded toward desert at a rate of more than 58 thousand square kilometers a year, meaning that in every 7 years an area the size of the state of California moves toward desert status (IUCN, 1977). These new deserts that are being created are not the biologically fascinating equivalent of the Mojave or Sonoran deserts, but true wastelands—desolate areas of rock and sand. Species that once inhabited the dry steppes and scrublands of the world are vanishing as those habitats are destroyed. Misplaced agriculture and excessive and mismanaged livestock are the principal factors behind desertification, aided of course by normally occurring dry years. According to the International Union for the Conservation of Nature (IUCN, 1978): "One of the most serious problems is the reduction in fertility, and often the outright loss of productive land. ... At current rates, the world will lose about one-third of its arable land between now and the end of the century—a period in which the human population will continue rapidly to increase." One can argue that human populations will not, in fact, increase if one-third of the arable land is lost, since starvation would take over.

These figures suggest that much of the present research and management effort on already well-studied species within the United States could be held in abeyance, with the experts now employed on this work being deployed instead to help with the desperate problems of the tropical world. Unfortunately, that would take an increased commitment of money for international assistance, an activity that presently would be a politically perilous move for any American government. Although we are willing in the United States to spend more than 200 billion dollars for military defense, we seem unwilling to commit funds to the planetary ecological defense, without which the military defense measures will end up being pointed the wrong way, at the wrong time, against the wrong enemy.

The changes in the natural communities of planet earth, now

being continually accelerated by human action, set in motion all the factors discussed earlier in this chapter. Tropical forests, for example, are not only exceedingly complex in numbers of species, they are intricately interwoven in food webs and distribution patterns. For example, Gilbert (1979) discusses "keystone mutualists" in tropical forests. These are defined as "those organisms, typically plants, which provide critical support to large complexes of mobile links." Mobile links, in turn, are those animals on which tropical plants depend for pollination (hummingbirds, bees, hawk moths, and bats) or seed dispersal (birds, bats, ants). The birds and bats involved in seed dispersal are mainly fruit eaters, whereas those engaged in pollination are the plant nectar feeders. An example of a keystone mutualist is the canopy tree, *Casearia corymbosa,* of neotropical forests. One bird, the masked tityra (*Tityra semifasciata*) is a principle seed disperser, but 21 other fruit-feeding birds use the trees. The tree supports several fruit eaters that depend on it during a critical period of fruit scarcity. Loss of this tree would therefore cause loss of several species that in turn are responsible for seed dispersal of a number of other fruit-bearing species of trees. Birds, bats, and flying insects serve to tie together great areas of forest within which individual trees of any one species are often widely scattered. The animals in turn depend on the sequential fruiting and flowering of a variety of trees for their support through the year, and must be able to move to areas where their food supply is currently available. Fragmentation of the forest through cutting and clearing breaks up these networks of plants and animals—another factor causing species extinction.

NATURE RESERVES

To save tropical forests, large reserves are required—much larger than most existing national parks. These reserves must be arranged in patterns that allow species to move between them, via protected corridors of vegetation, for example. The type of reserve that is needed would seem to be best satisfied by the *biosphere reserve* network that is being advocated, and slowly established, as part of UNESCO's Man and the Biosphere program (MAB). The MAB program, established and inadequately supported by those governments that belong to UNESCO, is an imaginative approach toward protecting the biosphere and its constituent ecosystems, while still encouraging economic development in the underdeveloped countries. However, the *biosphere reserve* network, intended to protect representative areas of the natural communities of the world, is somewhat too small in scope to accomplish the full task of species conservation that has recently become apparent. The biosphere reserves, ideally, contain a central area that is completely protected and reserved for scientific research or potentially for controlled, low-density visitation by the public. This central core reserve is surrounded by a buffer zone, also part of the total biosphere reserve. This buffer zone can be used for those forms of research that require disturbance or manipulation of the vegetation. It can also be used for limited and controlled sustainable cropping of resources, including hunting and fishing, as well as for more intensive recreational use. However, the general structure and species composition of the vegetation and animal life are maintained, so that the area interacts constantly with the core reserve. In this way, a much larger nature reserve can be estab-

These giraffe in the Tsavo National Park of Kenya are one of the many species that now largely depend on nature reserves for their continued survival.

lished than would be possible if the entire area had to be withdrawn from productive use or public recreation.

Unfortunately, most areas that have been proclaimed thus far as biosphere reserves fail to live up to this ideal. Those in North America are mostly areas that had already been protected as national parks or wildlife refuges and these do not yet have provision for either a completely protected core area, or a surrounding buffer zone, although they could be modified to meet these objectives. In fact, however, the western United States already had a reserve system that does meet, to a high degree, the ideal of a biosphere reserve. Olympic National Park, for example, which is a biosphere reserve, in combination with the surrounding multiple-use national forest (which is not included in the biosphere reserve) form a potential core and buffer area of the type required. One reason why the United States maintains a higher percentage of its original native wildlife, and in greater abundance than Europe, is that the fragmentation of habitat characteristic of Europe is avoided by the pattern of public land ownership. National parks and wilderness areas are commonly surrounded by national forest and these by lands of the original Public Domain, managed for multiple-use by the Bureau of Land Management. Although some of these lands are used intensively—for example, for timber production or grazing—and thus are modified from their original species composition, the entire complex maintains a pattern of natural vegetation and animal life that dominates the area west of the Rocky Mountains and occupies extensive tracts of land east of the Rockies. In this way, dangerous reductions in the size of natural communities is avoided. In California, with the greatest population of any state in the union, approximately half the land is included in federal reserves or their state counterparts. Much private land is also maintained in a near-natural condition and thus adds to the space available for wild species. It is probable that nothing less than a reserve system of this magnitude, including strictly protected areas, and carefully managed areas used for limited commodity production, is needed for the tropical world. At present, with the exception of Canada and perhaps the USSR, no other countries have come close to developing the necessary system of protected habitats.

ANIMAL TRADE

Although emphasis thus far has been placed on the necessity for a reserve system that will protect vegetation and animal habitat, this is not the only requirement for prevention of species extinction. An enormous amount of animal loss is still attributable directly to hunting or other kinds of killing, and some of this goes on as poaching inside national parks and other reserves. The problem of species loss can seldom be attributed to sport hunting, which is not an important activity in most countries, but to commercial and subsistence hunting. Commercial hunting, trapping, and trade in live animals, meat, hides, and other animal parts has been a business involving the exchange of billions of dollars. Its magnitude is seldom realized, since it is for most people invisible. In 1974, for example, Colombia exported 5 million dollars worth of hides and furs including jaguar, ocelot, margay, tiger cat, otter, giant otter, spectacled and black caimans (crocodilians), along with other species. Most of these are considered threatened species and to some degree are protected, on paper, within Colombia. In Thailand during 1967-1968 some "547,000 birds, 31,000 mammals, and 42,000 reptiles and amphibians were traded for a value of $1.9 million" (King, 1978). Most wildlife trade moves from tropical countries, the suppliers, to industrialized countries, the buyers.

"In 1968 before endangered species laws imposed new prohibitions on fur and hide imports, the U.S. fur industry imported about 1,300 Cheetah, 9,600 Leopard, 13,500 Jaguar, and 129,000 Ocelot skins with a combined declared value of $9.8 million. The industry also imported over 23 million skins of mink, sable, lynx, marten, lamb, beaver, rabbit, and other species having a declared value in excess of $100 million" (King, 1978). The demand for rhinoceros horn and elephant ivory represents a severe threat to these animals. With the price of ivory in 1976 at 35 dollars a pound, "at least 100,000 and maybe as many as 400,000 African elephants" were killed according to Iain Douglas-Hamilton (IUCN, 1977). Much of the elephant ivory moves from Africa and Southern Asia to markets in eastern Asia, via Hong Kong. There it is worked into carvings and re-exported to America and Europe.

In addition to animal hides, furs, and other products, there is a considerable trade in live wild animals, sold primarily as pets. All of this activity not only affects the animals actually captured or obtained dead, but also all the others which are wounded and escape, for an end result that at least seriously reduces populations and sometimes leads to local or more widespread extermination. It is virtually impossible to control this trade at the supply end, since the price of ivory or the 200 dollars offered for a leopard skin, can bring far more than a normal year's income to the local hunter. Efforts to control the trade at the purchaser's end have been more successful. These resulted in 1975 in the Convention on International Trade in Endangered Species, which, as more and more nations adhere to it is slowly reducing the flow of endangered or threatened species through the world's markets. It is, however, an uphill fight, since those engaged in illegal trade are adept at finding ways to circumvent enforcement of wildlife protective legislation.

INTERNATIONAL ASSISTANCE

Many organizations are engaged in efforts to protect wildlife internationally, and among the most noteworthy private or quasi-governmental groups are the International Union for the Conservation of Nature (IUCN), established by UNESCO in 1948, and its associate, the World Wildlife Fund, established through IUCN's efforts in 1951. These, along with the older International Committee for Bird Preservation, work in all countries but concentrate their efforts in countries that cannot afford to take the steps required for nature conservation from their own resources. Among the intergovernmental UN agencies, UNESCO through its Man and the Biosphere Programme, and FAO, through its Forestry and Fisheries Departments are most active on the ground. The United Nations Environment Programme, established in 1972, works with the older UN agencies, provides funds for the International Union for Conservation of Nature, and manages a number of environmental programs of its own that have conservation aspects. Much is accomplished, however, through direct government-to-government assistance, such as the Canadian international assistance program that helped maintain the Serengeti National Park in Tanzania. Much is also accomplished by universities and private agencies that devote money or send trained experts to work in developing countries. However, the total amount that is expended internationally in aid flowing from rich countries to poor countries is trivial compared to what is needed. The bulk of the expense and the full responsibility rests ultimately on the country directly concerned, and it is only the people of that country who will determine whether species conservation is to succeed or fail. The United States, for example, can do the most for the world by doing a first-rate job of nature conservation at home and publicizing its successes. But the United States must also, for the sake of its own long-term survival if nothing else, provide direct assistance to those other countries that need help toward maintaining their natural heritage of wildlife and wild country.

10

THE CONTROLLERS

Ownership and authority over wildlife in the United States still remains primarily in the 50 states and is exercised by state government agencies. All the states have a wildlife agency that does the work of conservation and management. For certain groups of species—migratory birds, endangered forms, and marine mammals, for example—the federal government has assumed a primary responsibility, but considerable authority remains with the states. The principal goal for any government wildlife agency, state or federal, is to *maintain viable populations of the wild species of America,* living so far as is possible, in their natural habitats. If that goal is accomplished, the agency can be given credit for having done its job well. It should not be considered a primary responsibility of a wildlife agency to keep the public happy, nor to satisfy the demands of various vocal sections of the public who happen to want to hunt, or to have all predators destroyed, or to have all animals everywhere treated with tender, loving care. If populations of coyotes and mountain lions, bighorn sheep and sage grouse, bobwhite, wild turkey, ivory-billed woodpeckers, condors, kangaroo rats, Bell's vireos, and Kirtland warblers are doing well, the wildlife agencies are doing well. If sheepmen or shooters are not pleased, that is, or should be, secondary. To the extent that we stray from that goal, American wildlife management agencies will be failing to safeguard the long-term interests of all the American people.

Having said that (and I cannot emphasize it too much), it is also necessary to consider other realities. Government agencies are part of government and governments are part of politics. No administration or legislature that displeases the voters of the United States can stay on the job for very long. No wildlife administrator who consistently annoys the sportsmen, the livestock owners, the bird-watchers, and other public interest groups can hold a job long enough to protect any species. Directors of state fish and game agencies, or the federal Fish and Wildlife Service, or the various fish and game commissions, must learn to be "fast on their feet" politically while always remaining on safe biological ground. Most of their time is not spent on wildlife populations, but on human problems—attempting to satisfy the wishes of the broadest segment of the human population while still protecting the interests of wildlife populations.

Since in most states the revenue for the support of most fish and wildlife conservation comes from licenses and other fees charged to sport hunters or fishers, commercial users of wildlife, and a variety of smaller groups who pay for the right to make some use of wild populations (game breeders, fish farmers, etc.), there was a tendency in the past for fish and game agencies to pay particular attention to the interests of these user groups. However, since public interest in wildlife, for its own sake, has grown, most, if not all, wildlife agencies now devote considerable attention to species that have no particular game or commercial value. Nevertheless, it is still the sport hunters and fishers who make up the most politically active body in support of wildlife in most states. If they are not happy with a wildlife agency, it is not difficult for them to go to the legislature and have the rules changed or the personnel of the agency removed from office. Fortunately, the politically organized hunters and fishers are usually conservation minded and have a strong interest in protecting the wildlife resources they use for their recreation. This is not usually true of those interest groups—farmers, foresters, and ranchers—who take the brunt of damage caused by wildlife.

In the first edition of this book I stated:

the responsibilities of the wildlife manager fall into two categories: the improvement of habitats to make them suitable for the maintenance of wildlife in abundance and variety and, secondly, the control of numbers of wild animals to keep them in balance with their habitat and avoid conflicts with other uses of the land. The first task often involves the use of an axe or tractor; the second involves the much more difficult job of managing people. Often there is no point in working to improve habitats unless provision can first be made to control the numbers of game that will be produced.

This statement now requires some modification and explanation.

During the 1950s and 1960s a sort of management madness infected many who were concerned with wildlife or wild-land resources. Productivity of wild land that was not channeled into the production of usable crops was considered wasted. Trees that were not cut, grasses that were not grazed, shrubs not browsed, unconsumed plankton, wildlife not harvested—all were regarded as "wasted resources." For the wildlife manager, the goal of maximum production of shootable or fishable game from minimum area would have been pursued if funds had been available. Maximum management for maximum yield was pursued, as far as possible, regardless of the fact that those wildlife managers who pursued it often sought the most remote areas for their own recreation, where their own efforts were least obvious and the wildlife showed least signs of management. The old Leopold rule that the recreational value of wildlife is inversely proportional to the management activity required to produce it seemed to have been forgotten. Fortunately, all-out management was not pursued, perhaps because the interested public were uncomfortable with the idea. Money to carry it out, except in limited areas, was generally not available, and still is not available.

During earlier decades the greatest emphasis by wildlife biologists and managers was placed on species populations: understanding them, increasing them, controlling them. Today the emphasis is shifting to ecosystems, not species, and the management of ecosystems is a much more subtle and difficult job. We know a great deal about producing more deer, pheasants, quail, ducks, geese. We know far less about maintaining balanced ecosystems with all of their natural components. Using fire, bulldozers, chemical sprays, and so on you can grow a lot of deer—but at the expense of creating unbalanced monocultures.

There are relatively few places in the United States that are or can be managed primarily for wildlife. Where they do exist, these lands are usually in the form of state or federal wildlife refuges, management areas, or conservation areas and may have been set aside or purchased to protect a particular species or group of species, or to provide public hunting or other outdoor recreation involving wildlife. These places can and should be managed intensively for wildlife production, or to maintain migratory populations on their resting or wintering grounds. However, most lands on which most wildlife species depend are not in this category. Most lands are in private ownership, and commonly the owner does not give wildlife conservation a high priority among the purposes for which he or she uses and manages the land. There are exceptions, of course: private hunting clubs or estates, or private wildlife reserves that are used primarily to produce or protect wildlife. Most privately owned lands, other than those that are purely residential, are used principally for agriculture, livestock grazing, or timber production. In the past these areas have had important secondary values for maintaining wildlife populations. In more recent years there has been a trend in the opposite direction.

George Burger has reviewed the present status of wildlife on agricultural lands, and has noted a general decline in abundance and variety. Even the ring-necked pheasant, a species well adapted to farming lands, has difficulty surviving on the monocultural crop lands of the nation. In the past agriculture was diversified, and there was plenty of waste space for wildlife to fit in, but this is no longer generally true. The high prices paid for agricultural crops, and the exceedingly high cost of mechanized farming, with heavy inputs of fertilizers, irrigation water, pesticides, and other chemicals, forces most farmers to use even relatively marginal land. The massive equipment now used on large farms does not operate well on land with hedgerows, or food patches for wildlife. The loss of diversification and cover alone would reduce wildlife populations. The heavy use of pesticides contributes further to the problem. Burger points out that:

Thus much of today's cropland has undergone a major loss of wildlife species diversity and, in places, a loss of almost all wildlife, even the most adaptable. It is true that modern agriculture provides certain crops and waste grains that waterfowl and other wildlife use. It is also true that these real or apparent benefits may prove ephemeral, vanishing with changes in farm technology and land use, and that they have almost always replaced stable natural habitats and food sources.

Looking to the future, Burger states: "Continuation of the present trends which are geared primarily to short-term profits and goals would inevitably result in greater conflicts with wildlife and other natural resources. Increasing problems with pests and wildlife depredations are inevitable with increasing monoculture.

No room for wild animals.

Farmers will call for new and more pesticides. . . . The loss of contact between the farmer and his land will continue."

Burger does suggest an agricultural direction that would prevent the continued decline, a return to smaller farms, diversified planting, re-use of those soil conservation measures that have been abandoned, an expansion of organic farming with recycling of municipal sludge and garbage. Appeals for such a balanced, sustainable, conservation agriculture have had little effect in the past. Today, however, with the high cost of petroleum, some shift in agricultural direction seems likely. A return of farmers to the farms, taking the land back from agribusiness, would give new hope to wildlife.

On the nation's rangelands there has also been a tendency toward emphasizing increases in production and yield of livestock forage at the expense of species diversity. However, on the drier range lands, the economics of land improvement still favor wildlife. It does not pay, even with high meat prices, to put much money into intensive forage production, except on irrigated pastures. Rangelands remain in a relatively wild state, diversified and with considerable wildlife variety. James Teer and his colleagues have examined the situation in the western portion of the Edward's Plateau in Texas, a prime habitat for white-tailed deer. He believes that three socioeconomic factors must be considered in management plans for deer in that region: "(1) the economic value of deer to landowners, (2) the protection of the range resources, and (3) the demands for hunting recreation by sportsmen." In Texas, with few exceptions, land is privately owned. Landowners are also permitted to charge fees for hunting on their land, which can make it economically attractive for them to maintain wildlife. Teer *et al.* point out that the landowners (1) control the deer range and, therefore, the deer herd, (2) their interest in deer, while partly aesthetic is primarily related to the herd's economic value, and (3) the present system of management, whereby deer are "produced," "owned," and "sold," offers the highest probability for perpetuating the herd and the greatest potential for providing the greatest amount of hunting recreation. Unless a drastic change occurs in traditions and current laws governing private ownership of property, any other approach to management would be unrealisitc."

Elsewhere in the United States, rights of landowners over the wildlife on their land are not so clearly established. Nevertheless, by charging trespass fees, or other means, it has been possible for owners of grazing lands to obtain some income from wildlife. This at least enables them to tolerate the conflict for forage between deer, antelope, or elk, and their own livestock. However, even where the economic value of wildlife can be directly realized by the landowner, as on various African game ranches, there is strong pressure to favor an increase of livestock at the expense of wild animals.

The decline of large wild animals in the western United States has been related to and accompanied by an increase in numbers of domestic livestock. Overgrazing of ranges by livestock has in turn decreased their carrying capacity for both wildlife and livestock. In Fred Wagner's words:

A large part of the West has moved toward an impoverished landscape for both wildlife and livestock by growing up to overmature, depauperate stands of juniper, sage, shadscale, creosote, mesquite, and other species of low or no palatability. Judicious brush removal accompanied by seeding to native grasses and desirable shrubby species, could increase both wildlife habitat and livestock forage. Attention would be given to proper patterning and dispersion to achieve desirable wildlife habitat and landscape forms.

On severely degraded sites, more intensive management might be needed, including rodent control. At this level of effort, native perennial grass production has been increased fourfold on the almost totally destroyed desert grassland of southern New Mexico (Wagner, 1977). Once healthy grass stands were restored no further rodent control would be needed, the vegetation maintaining itself in the presence of these animals as it must have in presettlement times.

Although Wagner holds out hope that an overall improvement for both livestock and wildlife can be accomplished on western range lands, the present danger is that with increasing world demands for food, and the high cost of energy, much greater effort will be directed toward producing more livestock on western grazing lands. This could bring an effort to improve ranges and increase their carrying capacity, but not for the benefit of wildlife—an effort most likely to occur on private grazing lands.

As a result of continued heavy grazing a large part of the West has moved toward an impoverished landscape.

Privately owned forest lands have also moved from an era in which the relatively low price of forest products encouraged a lax attitude toward land management, to one in which the high price of timber encourages intensive forest management. Theoretically, good forest management should benefit all species, but the modern trend in forestry is toward high-yielding monocultures of fast-growing tree varieties. To produce these high yields, all potential competitors are removed, and use of herbicides, insecticides, fungicides, and rodenticides has become common. All are likely to have directly damaging effects on wildlife. In Starker Leopold's words:

> *Perhaps the most widespread forest practice—and one of least benefit to wildlife—is the culture of conifers, in pure, even-aged stands. In many situations, such stands are the highest yielding form of forest management. In the Southeast, an ever increasing acreage of pines is producing the pulp needed for paper mills. Large blocks are clearcut and planted densely to*

pure stands of the southern pine species. Growth is remarkably rapid and the trees are ready to feed into the chipper as early as 20 to 25 years after planting. But the utility of such a stand to birds and mammals is minimal. For a few years after planting, certain open-land species can make tempo-rary use of a new plantation, but before colonization can really get under-way, the canopy closes. In the lake states, an increasing acreage is planted densely to Jack Pine for pulp or Red Pine for logs. Among the most intensively managed forest areas in the country is the Douglas-fir zone in the Pacific Northwest where a great deal of forest land is devoted to the culture of fast growing, even-aged stands of Douglas-fir. The Redwood region of northern California is maintained in dense, fully stocked stands with little attractiveness to wildlife. Even the Ponderosa Pine, fir, and spruce forests of the Rocky Mountains and Sierra Nevada are being con-verted locally from mixed ages to even-aged plantations. Where fires or past cuts have exposed extensive areas of bare soil, the tendency on public as well as private lands is to plant the openings to conifers, thereby accel-erating reforestation and full stocking.

Through such processes the normal benefits of forest suc-cesion to wildlife are reduced or lost, and at the same time the old-growth forests that supported their own array of species, spotted owls and pileated woodpeckers among them, are on their way out, and not likely to return to privately owned timber lands. A great responsibility for the future of wildlife therefore falls upon the managers of public lands, where the people have the right to see that the future of wildlife will be safeguarded.

The public lands amount to over 760 million acres in the United States, with the greatest area in Alaska and the western states (Table 10.1). According to Gustav Swanson: "Without these lands, the future of wildlife in the United States would be very grim for the onslaught of *Homo sapiens* is expected to continue."

In addition to the federally owned lands, nearly 40 million acres of wildlife habitat are owned and managed by state govern-ments, according to data gathered by Swanson, which are admit-tedly incomplete (Table 10.2). There are in total more than 800 million acres of public land with some potential for wildlife con-servation. Two agencies, however, control the greatest area of land: the Bureau of Land Management and the Forest Service, which administer and manage nearly 660 million acres of land.

**Table 10.1   Federal Lands in the United States Administered by
Major Land Management Agencies as of June 30, 1975.**

Agency	Total Acres (Millions)	Natural Areas and Wilderness	
		Number	Acres (Millions)
Bureau of Land Management	470.2	35	2.4
Forest Service	187.5	224	11.9
Department of Defense	30.8	15	0.3
Fish and Wildlife Service	30.3	234	4.2
National Park Service	25.1	66	19.7
Others	17.0	6	0.4
Total Federal Lands	760.4	580	39.9

Source: Adapted from Swanson (1978)

Both are charged with managing their lands with a view to "multiple use," including timber yield, range forage production, watershed protection, outdoor recreation and fish and wildlife conservation. Their lands are also subject to the Mining Law of 1872, which makes their mineral resources available to private exploitation under certain conditions, and to the Mineral Leasing Act of 1920, which makes other categories of minerals available for private use under contract with the government.

From the viewpoint of wildlife, it is unfortunate that the Bureau of Land Management in its early history was forced by political considerations to concentrate primarily on livestock grazing and mining, and that these forms of use still dominate the Bureau's activities. By contrast, the Forest Service started its administrative life with a much more balanced conservation mandate. But the depletion of timber on private lands has led to greater pressure on the Forest Service to manage its lands for timber production. The result is that wildlife production receives relatively little attention from either agency. According to Swanson:

Table 10.2   State Owned Lands Providing Wildlife Habitat

	Number of units	Acres in thousands
Areas managed specifically for wildlife	5,236	11,321
Natural areas	840	925
Forests, parks, etc.	3,044	27,761
Total wildlife habitat	9,120	39,851

Source: Adapted from Swanson (1978)

More money alone will not solve the problems either. It takes qualified, dedicated, imaginative, and inspired staffs as well. But we have seen that in the Forest Service and the BLM, both multiple use agencies where wildlife and recreation should have equal standing with timber and grazing under the law, the budgets contain a pitiful 1.6 percent and 1 percent respectively, for the wildlife work. And the National Parks, with tremendous increases in visitors, have been less and less adequately staffed.

If this brief review suggests that the overall future for wildlife in the United States is not particularly bright, the suggestion is intended. However, the situation in this country is hopeful. The wildlife, for the most part, is still with us and conditions for it can be improved and numbers restored. We do not have to go the direction of single-purpose use of lands, which could result in the exclusion of wildlife. To avoid this, however, those to whom wildlife is important must play an active political role. Those wishing to exploit land for their own private benefit never cease their political efforts. Those who would protect the natural world cannot afford to do less.

It has been stated earlier that the idea of a surplus or waste in natural ecosystems does not reflect ecological reality. Timber that is not cut does not "go to waste"; it remains to supply a whole complex of organisms and to circulate its nutrients, eventually, back into the system. In natural systems all is used by all and a reduction in any one component affects all others. This does not mean that there is no sustainable yield. It may mean that the yields that we have thought sustainable—particularly in forestry, fisheries, agriculture, and more intensive forms of livestock production—may not in fact be sustainable for the long run. Any drain of materials from an ecosystem that exceeds the rate at which those materials are replaced will lead in time to depletion and degradation of the system. The rate of depletion may be slow and not noticeable in the short run. It is the long run that must be considered.

N. Stark has reported on the "biological life of a soil," which he defines as "the geologic time in years that a particular soil can support a forest in forest climate" or, presumably, other ecosystems in other climates. He discusses the problem of nutrient drains that exceed the rate of soil formation from decomposition of rock and addition of nutrients from the atmosphere or other sources. He found that Montana soils, subjected to relatively mild nutrient drains resulting from wildfires at 50-year intervals, could hold up for 55,000 years. However, since "any biological life spanning over 500 to 1000 years will intercept geologic, major erosional, glacial, successional, climatic, and other cycles which are beyond our control" such a 55,000 year span can be regarded in human terms as "forever." He did not examine the biological life of such soils under continued assault from intensive harvesting on some theoretical "maximum sustainable" basis. For the white sand soils that are common in the humid tropics, however, he found a biological life span of 90 to 240 years, after which the soils would become essentially sterile. Such a lifespan is of immediate and serious concern. A heavy removal of materials could finish off such soils in a short period of time. Low remaining biological lives can also be found in old, long-weathered soils elsewhere, and also new soils subjected to heavy nutrient losses. Thin soils over talus slopes, permafrost, or poor granite are likely to be vulnerable. Sudden loss of essential elements that happen to be in short supply can remove them from productive capacity over hundreds or thousands of years (Stark, 1978).

Sport hunting and fishing rarely occur at a rate likely to cause serious nutrient removal over the foreseeable future. However, they can cause important shifts in the species composition of ecosystems, and these shifts must be taken into account in any area where heavy hunting or intensive management is considered. With the complex of laws and regulations now in effect, however, the wildlife of the United States appears to be protected adequately against the effects of sport hunting. Sport hunters and fishers are rarely a part of wildlife problems—usually they are a part of the solution. Those who hunt and those who do not must join forces, if the real problems associated with habitat destruction are to be solved. Solutions are possible in the United States, and in Canada, in northern and western Europe, in the USSR, Australia and New Zealand, and a few other places without any sacrifice in the economic "standard of living" or other indicators of economic well-being. In other parts of the world it is much more difficult, and hard choices must be considered.

It can be argued that it would be more important to protect an area of Amazonia the size of North and South Dakota, and allow all of the wildlife of the Dakotas to perish, instead of protecting the Dakotas and allowing all the wildlife in that Amazonian area to die off. Ecologically, and in terms of the richness and variety of wild species, the Amazonian area would have to be considered more important. We do not have to face that choice yet. Nevertheless, because of the shortage of available money, trained personnel, and the general willingness of governments and people to commit themselves to conservation, just that sort of choice is now forced on the organizations involved in international conservation. Their funds are limited. Where should they be spent? It is more important biologically perhaps to protect a viable population of manatees or dugongs, the last members of the order Sirenia on earth, than to protect the last wolves, even if wolves were the last members of the family Canidae on earth. If all Canids died there would still be other members of the order Carnivora alive. If all Sirenians died there would be nothing at all like them left on earth. From the same point of view it would be more worthwhile creating and protecting a national park or biosphere reserve in western Colombia or southern Algeria than creating and protecting another reserve in East Africa. One area has none, the other many. We should not have to make such dire decisions to sacrifice major segments of the living fabric of this planet. But we are making them deliberately, or through inaction, every day. Unless people and the governments they support can be made to understand the importance of conserving the biological diversity of the earth, those of us who are committed to the conservation of wildlife can only use our scarce resources to the best possible advantage.

During the time between the writing of this book and its publication, another 42,000 square miles of tropical forest will have been cut down, another 22,000 square miles of once productive land will have become desert. All the species that lived in those areas will have been killed off, or moved out—to where? What can you do about it? Only you can make that decision. Some do nothing. Some give a little money and a little time, which helps. Some give their lives.

REFERENCES

Aldous, Shaler E. (1952). Deer browse clipping study in the Lake States region. *Jour. Wildl. Mgmt.,*16: 401–409.

Allee, W. C. (1931). *Animal aggregations.* University of Chicago Press, Chicago.

Allen, Durward (1943). *Michigan fox squirrel management.* Mich. Dept. Cons. Game Div. Publ. 100, 404 pp.

Anderson, J. (1953). Analysis of a Danish roe-deer population. Danish Rev. Game Biol., 2: 127–155.

Baker, Herbert (1970) Evolution in the tropics. *Biotropica,* 2: 101–111.

Banfield, A. W. F. (1954). *Preliminary investigations of the barren-ground caribou.* Wildl. Mgmt. Bull. Series 1, No. 10 A -B, Dept. Northern Affairs and National Resources, Ottawa.

Bellrose, F. C. (1958) Celestial orientation by wild mallards. *Bird-banding,* 29: 75–90.

Bergerud, Arthur T. (1971). The population dynamics of Newfoundland caribou. *Wildl. Monographs,* 25.

Bissell H. D. and H. Strong (1955). The crude protein variation in the browse diet of California deer. *Calif. Fish and Game,* 41: 145–155.

Bourliere, F. and J. Verschuren (1960). *Introduction à l'écologie des ongules du Parc National Albert.* Inst. des Parcs Nationaux du Congo Belge, Bruxelles.

Bourliere, F. (1962). The uniqueness of African big game fauna. *African Wild Life,* 16: 95–100.

Boyle, C. L. (1961). Nature conservation in Poland. *Oryx,* 6: 6–26.

Brand, C. J., L. B. Keith, and C. A. Fischer (1976). Lynx responses to changing snowshoe hare densities in Central Alberta. *Jour. Wildl. Mgmt.,* 40: 416–428.

Brewer, Richard (1979). *Principles of ecology.* W. B. Saunders, Philadelphia.

Brokaw, Howard P., Ed. (1978). *Wildlife and America.* Council on Environmental Quality, Washington, D.C.

Brooks, Maurice (1955). An isolated population of Virginia varying hare. *Jour. Wildl. Mgmt.,* 19: 61-64.

Buechner, Helmut K. (1960). The bighorn sheep in the United States, its past, present and future. *Wildl. Monographs,* 4.

Burger, George V. (1978). Agriculture and wildlife. In Brokaw, Howard P. (ed.),*Wildlife and America.* pp. 89-107.

Calhoun, John B. (1952). The social aspects of population dynamics. *Jour. Mammalogy,* 33: 139-159.

Caughley, Graeme (1977). *Analysis of vertebrate populations.* John Wiley-Interscience, London.

Chase, W. W. and D. H. Jenkins (1962). Productivity of the George Reserve deer herd. *Proc. National White-tailed deer disease symposium,* 1: 78-88.

Christian, J. J. (1950). The adreno-pituitary system and population cycles in mammals. *Jour. Mammalogy,* 31: 246-260.

Croon, G. W., D. R. McCullough, C. E. Olsen, and L. M. Queal (1968). Infrared scanning techniques for big-game census. *Jour. Wildl. Mgmt.,* 32: 751-759.

Curry-Lindahl, Kai (1970). The brown bear (*Ursus arctos* L.) in Europe: decline, present distribution, biology and ecology. pp. 74-80 in *Bears—their biology and management.* IUCN New Series, 23. Morges, Switzerland.

Dasmann, R. F. (1964). *African game ranching.* Pergamon Press, Oxford.

——and A. S. Mossman (1962). Abundance and population structure of wild ungulates in some areas of Southern Rhodesia. *Jour. Wildl. Mgmt.* 26: 262-268.

——and A. S. Mossman (1962). Reproduction in some ungulates in Southern Rhodesia. *Jour. Mammalogy* 43: 533-537.

Dasmann, W. P. (1945). A method for estimating carrying capacity of range lands. *Jour. Forestry,* 43: 400-407.

——(1971). *If deer are to survive.* Wildlife Management Institute. Stackpole, Harrisburg, Pa.

Davison, Verne. E. (1940). An 8-year census of lesser prairie chickens. *Jour. Wildl. Mgmt.,* 4: 55-62.

Diamond, Jared M. (1979). Patchy distribution of tropical birds. *Conservation Biology,* Sinauer Assoc., Sunderland, Mass. 57-74.

Dice, Lee R. (1943). *The biotic provinces of North America.* University of Michigan Press, Ann Arbor.

Eckholm, Eric P. (1976). *Losing ground.* Worldwatch Institute. W. W. Norton, New York.

Edminister, F. C. (1939). The effect of predator control on ruffed grouse populations in New York. *Jour. Wildl. Mgmt.,* 3: 345-352.

Edwards, R. Y. and C. D. Fowle (1955). The concept of carrying capacity. *Trans. North American Wildlife Conf.* 20:589-602.

Ellison, Lincoln (1954). Subalpine vegetation of the Wasatch Plateau, Utah. *Ecol. Monographs,* 24: 89-184.

Elton, Charles (1942). *Voles, mice and lemmings.* Oxford, London.
————and M. Nicholson (1942). The ten-year cycle in numbers of lynx in Canada. *Jour. Animal Ecol.,* 11: 215-244.

Emmel, Thomas C. (1973). *An introduction to ecology and population biology.* W. W. Norton, New York.

Errington, Paul L. (1945). Some contributions of a 15-year study of the northern bobwhite to a knowledge of population phenomena. *Ecol. Monographs,* 15: 1-34.
————(1954). On the hazards of overemphasizing numerical fluctuations in studies of "cyclic" phenomena in muskrat populations. *Jour. Wildl. Mgmt.,* 18: 66-90.

Evans, H. (1891) *Some account of Jura red deer.* Francis Carter, Derby, England.

Fitch, John E. (1974). *Offshore fishes of California.* Calif. Dept. of Fish and Game, Sacramento.

Fittkau, E. J. and H. Klinge (1973). On biomass and trophic structure of the Central Amazonian rain forest ecosystem. *Biotropica,* 5: 2-14.

Frank, Fritz (1957). The causality of microtine cycles in Germany. *Jour. Wildl. Mgmt.,* 21: 113-121.

Fraser Darling, Frank (1938). *Bird flocks and the breeding cycle.* Cambridge University Press, Cambridge.

French, C. E., L. C. McEwen, N. D. Magruder, R. H. Ingram and R. W. Swift (1956). Nutrient requirements for growth and antler development in the white-tailed deer. *Jour. Wildl. Mgmt.* 20: 221-232.

Fuller, W. A. (1962). The biology and management of the bison of Wood Buffalo National Park. *Wildl. Mgmt. Bull.* Series 1, No. 16. Canadian Wildlife Service, Ottawa.

Gause, G. F. (1934). *The struggle for existence.* Williams and Wilkins, Baltimore.

Gilbert, Lawrence E. (1979). Conservation of neotropical diversity. *Conservation Biology,* Sinauer Assoc., Sunderland, Mass. 11-34.

Graham, Edward H. (1947). *The land and wildlife.* Oxford, New York.

Grange, W. B. (1948). *Wisconsin grouse problems.* Wisconsin Cons. Dept. Publ. 328.

Green, R. G., C. L. Larson, and J. F. Bell (1939). Shock disease as the cause of the periodic decimation of the snowshoe hare. *Amer. Jour. Hygiene,* 30 (B): 83-102.

Green, R. G. and C. A. Evans (1940). Studies on a population cycle of snowshoe hares in the Lake Alexander area. *Jour. Wildl. Mgmt.,* 4: 220-238, 267-278, 347-358.

Grinnell, Joseph (1943). *Philosophy of nature.* University of California Press, Berkeley.

Hamilton, W. J. III (1962). Celestial orientation in juvenal waterfowl. *Condor,* 64:19-33.

Haynes, R. W. (1949). Calculation of size of home range. *Jour. Mammalogy,* 30: 1-18.

Heady, Harold (1960). *Range management in East Africa.* Government Printer, Nairobi.

Hewitt, Oliver H., Ed. (1954). A symposium on cycles in animal populations. *Jour. Wildl. Mgmt.,* 18: 1-112.

Hornocker, M. G. (1969). Winter territoriality in mountain lions. *Jour. Wildl. Mgmt.* 33: 457-464.

Howard, H. E. (1920). *Territory in bird life.* E. P. Dutton and Co., New York.

Hudson, W. H. (1903). *The naturalist in La Plata.* J. M. Dent, London.

Humbert, John and W. P. Dasmann (1945). Range management—a restatement of definition and objectives. *Jour. Forestry,* 43: 263-264.

IUCN (1977). *IUCN Bulletin.* Vol. 8: 43-58, 65-70. IUCN, Morges, Switzerland.

————(1978). *A world conservation strategy.* First Draft. IUCN, Morges, Switzerland.

Jonkel, C. J., G. B. Kolenosky, R. J. Robertson, and R. H. Russell (1970). Further notes on polar bear denning habits. pp. 142-158 in *Bears—their biology and management.* IUCN New Series, No. 23.

Keith, Lloyd B. (1962). *Wildlife's ten-year cycle.* University of Wisconsin Press, Madison.

Kimball, Thomas and Raymond Johnson (1978). The richness of American wildlife. pp. 3-17 in Brokaw, H., ed., *Wildlife and America,* Council on Environmental Quality, Washington, D.C.

King, F. Wayne (1978). The wildlife trade. pp 253-272 in Brokaw, H., ed. *Wildlife and America,* Council on Environmental Quality, Washington, D.C.

Koford, Carl (1957). The vicuna and the puna. *Ecol. Monographs,* 27: 153-219.

————(1958). Prairie dogs, whitefaces, and blue grama. *Wildlife Monographs,* 3.

Kozicky, E. L.; G. O. Hendrickson, P. G. Homyer (1955). Weather and fall pheasant populations in Iowa. *Jour. Wildl. Mgmt.* 19: 136-142.

Lack, David (1954). *The natural regulation of animal numbers.* Oxford, Clarendon Press, London.

Leopold, Aldo (1933). *Game managment.* Charles Scribner's, New York.

————(1949). *A Sand County Almanac.* Oxford, New York.

Leopold, A. S., M. Erwin, J. Oh, and B. Browning (1976). Phytoestrogens: adverse effects on reproduction in California quail. *Science,* 191: 98-100.

Leopold, A. Starker (1978). Wildlife and forest practice. pp. 108-120 in Brokaw, H., ed. *Wildlife and America,* Council on Environmental Quality, Washington, D.C.

Lincoln, F. C. (1951). *Migration of birds.* Circ. 16, United States Fish and Wildlife Service, Washington, D.C.

Longhurst, William, A. S. Leopold, and R. F. Dasmann (1952). *A survey of California deer herds, their ranges and management problems.* Game Bull. 6, California Dept of Fish and Game, Sacramento.

Lydekker, R. (1898). *Wild oxen, sheep and goats of all lands.* Rowland Ward, London.

MacArthur, R. H., and E. O. Wilson (1967). *The theory of island biogeography.* Princeton University Press, Princeton, N.J.

Margolin, Malcolm (1978). *The Ohlone way.* Heyday Books, Berkeley.

May, Robert M., J. R. Beddington, C. W. Clark, S. J. Holt, and R. M. Laws (1979). Management of multispecies fisheries. *Science,* 205: 267-277.

McLuhan, T. C. (1972). *Touch the earth.* Pocket Books, New York.

Meagher, Margaret M. (1973). *The bison of Yellowstone National Park.* National Park Service Scientific Monograph Series, No. 1.

Mech, L. David (1970) *The wolf.* Natural History Press, New York.

Medin, Dean E. and Allen E. Anderson (1979). Modeling the dynamics of a Colorado mule deer population. *Wildl. Monographs,* 68.

Merriam, H. R., 1964. The wolves of Coronation Island. *Proc. Alaska Science Conference,* 15: 27-32.

Miller, R. S. and D. B. Botkin (1974). Endangered species: models and predictions. *American Scientist,* 62: 172-181.

Murie, Adolf (1944). The wolves of Mount McKinley. U. S. Dept. Interior, National Park Service, *Fauna of the National Parks of the United States.* Fauna Series 5.

Nice, Margaret (1941). The role of territory in bird life. *American Midland Naturalist,* 26: 441-487.

Odum, Eugene P. (1972). *Fundamentals of ecology.* 3rd ed. W. B. Saunders, Philadelphia.

O'Roke, E. C. and F. N. Hamerstrom (1948). Productivity and yield of the George Reserve deer herd. *Jour Wildl. Mgmt.,* 12: 78-86.

Palmer, W. L. (1956). Ruffed grouse population studies on hunted and unhunted areas. *Trans. North American Wildlife Conf.,* 21: 338-345.

Pearl, Raymond and L. J. Reed (1920). On the rate of growth of the population of the United States since 1790 and its mathematical representation. *Proc. National Academy of Science,* 6: 275-288.

Pitelka, F. A. (1957). Some characteristics of microtine cycles in the Arctic. *18th Biol. Colloqium, Proceedings.* Oregon State University, pp. 73-88.

Pitelka, F. A. (1959). Population studies of lemmings and lemming predators in northern Alaska. 15th International Congress of Zoology, Sect. X, Paper 5.

Rasmussen, D. I. (1941). Biotic communities of the Kaibab plateau. *Ecol. Monographs,* 3: 229-275.

Ratcliffe, F. N. (1959). The rabbit in Australia. *Biogeography and Ecology in Australia.* Monog. Biol. 8: 545-564.

Ripely, S. Dillon and T. E. Lovejoy (1978). Threatened and endangered species. pp. 365-378 in Brokaw, H., ed., *Wildlife and America.* Council on Environmental Quality, Washington, D.C.

Risebrough, Robert W. (1978). Pesticides and other toxicants. pp. 218-236 in Brokaw, H., ed., *Wildlife and America* Council on Environmental Quality, Washington, D.C.

Rusch, D. H. and L. B. Keith (1971). Seasonal and annual trends in numbers of Alberta ruffed grouse. *Jour. Wildl. Mgmt.,* 35: 803-822.

Salwasser, Hal (1979). *The ecology and management of the Devil's Garden interstate deer herd and its range.* Ph. D. dissertation, College of Natural Resources, University of California, Berkeley.

Scheffer, Victor B. (1951). The rise and fall of a reindeer herd. *Scientific Monthly,* 73: 356-362.

Sclater, P. L. (1858). On the general geographical distribution of the members of the class Aves. *Jour. Proc. Linnaean Soc.* (Zool.), 2: 130-145.

Seidensticker, John C. M. G. Hornocker, W. V. Wiles and J. P. Messick (1973). Mountain lion social organization in the Idaho Primitive Area. *Wildl. Monographs,* 35.

Seton, Ernest Thompson (1923). *The arctic prairies.* Charles Scribner's, New York.

Shane, Douglas R., ed. (1978). *Tropical deforestation.* Proceedings of the U. S. Strategy Conference, Dept. of State, Washington, D.C.

Shortridge, G. C. (1934). *The mammals of Southwest Africa.* Heinemann, London.

Snyder, Gary (1977). *The old ways.* City Lights Books, San Francisco.

Stark, N. (1978). Man, tropical forests, and the biological life of a soil. *Biotropica,* 10: 1-10.

Stevenson-Hamilton, J. (1912). *Animal life in Africa.* E. P. Dutton, New York.

Strandgaard, B. H. (1972). The roe deer *(Capreolus capreolus)* population at Kalø and the factors regulating its size. *Danish Rev. Game Biol.* 7: 1-205.

Stubblebine, W., J. H. Langenheim and D. Lincoln (1978). Vegetative response to photoperiod in the tropical leguminous tree *Hymenaea courbaril* L. *Biotropica,* 10: 18-29.

Swanson, Gustav A. (1978). Wildlife on the public lands. pp. 428-441 in *Wildlife and America,* H. Brokaw, ed., Council on Environmental Quality, Washington, D.C.

Taber, R. D. and R. F. Dasmann (1957). The dynamics of three natural populations of the deer *Odocoileus hemionus columbianus. Ecology,* 38: 233-246.

Taber, R. D. and R. F. Dasmann (1958). *The black-tailed deer of the chaparral.* Calif. Dept. of Fish and Game, Game Bull. 8.

Talbot, Lee M. and Martha H. (1963). The wildebeest in western Masailand, East Africa. *Wildl. Monographs,* 12.

Teer, James G.; J. W. Thomas and E. A. Walker (1965). Ecology and management of white-tailed deer in the Llano Basin of Texas. *Wildl. Monographs,* 15.

Terborgh, Jon and Blair Winter (1979). Some causes of extinction. *Conservation Biology,* Sinauer Assoc., Sunderland, Mass. 119-134.

Udvardy, Miklos (1975). *A classification of the biogeographical provinces of the world.* IUCN Occasional Paper 18, Morges, Switzerland.

Wagner, Frederic H. (1978). Livestock grazing and the livestock industry. pp. 121-145 in Brokaw, H., ed., *Wildlife and America.* Council on Environmental Quality, Washington, D.C.

Wallace, Alfred Russell (1876). *The geographic distribution of animals.* Macmillan, London.

Watson, A. and R. Moss (1970). Dominance, spacing behavior and aggression in relation to population limitation in vertebrates. pp. 167–220 in Watson, A., ed., *Animal populations in relation to their food resources.* Blackwell Scientific Publications, Oxford.

Willis, E. O. (1974). Population and local extinctions of birds on Barro Colorado Island, Panama. *Ecol. Monographs,* 44:153–169.

Wilson, E. O. (1971). Competition and aggressive behavior. pp. 181–217 in Eisenberg, J. F. and W. S. Dillon, eds., *Man and Beast.* Smithsonian Institution, Washington.

Wodzicki, K. (1961). Ecology and management of introduced ungulates in New Zealand. *La terre et la vie,* 1: 130–157.

Wood, A. J., I. M. Cowan, and H. C. Nordan (1962). Periodicity of growth in ungulates as shown by deer of the genus *Odocoileus. Canadian Jour. Zool.,* 40: 593–603.

Woolf, Alan and J. D. Harder (1979). Population dynamics of a captive white-tailed deer herd with emphasis on reproduction and mortality. *Wildl. Monographs,* 67.

PHOTO CREDITS

Chapter 1
Opener: Hugh M. Halliday/Photo Trends. 6: Georg Gerster/Photo Researchers. 16: Gene Daniels/EPA-Documerica.
Chapter 2
Opener: Paul Lambert/WHO. 23: Bryan Alexander/Photo Trends. 26: Arthur H. Bilsten/The National Audubon Society Collection-Photo Researchers.
Chapter 3
Opener: Jacques Lang/Rapho-Photo Researchers. 36: Normann Poltlethwaite/USDA-SCS. 42: Charles O'Rear/EPA-Documerica. 44: Africa pix/Peter Arnold.
Chapter 4
Opener: Donald Paterson/Coleman & Hayward/Photo Researchers. 61: U.S.S. Forest Service. 69: Forsythe/USDA.
Chapter 5
Opener: Jen and Des Bartlett/Photo Researchers. 88: Morris Huberland/The National Audubon Society Collection-Photo Researchers.
Chapter 6
Opener: National Film Board of Canada. 106: Harry Engels/The National Audubon Society Collection-Photo Researchers.
Chapter 7
Opener: National Film Board of Canada. 128: Bayliss & Botting/Photo Trends. 147: Carl Koford/The National Audubon Society Collection-Photo Researchers.
Chapter 8
Opener: Jim Yoakum. 157: U.S. Forest Service.
Chapter 9
Opener: B. Revenko/Novosti from Sovfoto. 172: Georg Gerster/Rapho-Photo Researchers. 175: Mary M. Thacher/Photo Researchers.
Chapter 10
Opener: USDA. 185: Cornelius Keyes/EPA-Documerica. 188: U.S. Forest Service.

INDEX